# PRAISE FOᴿ

"I read this book in one sitting and immediately went back to revisit pages—it resonated that deeply. *Creating a Salon* goes far beyond the useful tips and templates; it's a beautiful invitation to meaningful connection in a world that too often settles for small talk. Linda-Marie Barrett writes with warmth, wisdom, and heart, offering not just a guide to create intentional gatherings, but a gentle reminder of our shared human need to be seen, heard, and held in community. This book feels like a warm hug and a spark of inspiration all at once. I'll recommend it to every book club leader, every book-loving friend, and anyone who hosts (or hopes to host) spaces that truly matter."

> —SHARI STAUCH, owner and founder of Main Street Reads

"Linda-Marie Barrett's *Creating a Salon* could not have come at a better time. As a bookstore owner who prioritizes meaningful connection with and among our community members, this book will help me structure group conversations we ourselves host."

> —JANET GEDDIS, owner and founder of Avid Bookshop

"Whether you are in a book club that could use a boost, want to deepen relationships with friends, or are interested in starting your own salon, this is the book you need. It's that rare combination of inspiring and immensely useful. Linda-Marie Barrett guides us through every aspect of setting up and leading a salon and includes anecdotes and candid feedback from long-time members. Some stories brought me to tears and others made me vow to try new ways of living and connecting."

> —SARAH GODDIN, McIntyre's Book

"Reading *Creating a Salon: The Magic of Conversations That Matter* feels like entering a sacred space—one that captures the quiet power of gathering with intention, where those who enter are met with curiosity, warmth, and grace. Author Linda-Marie Barrett draws on her experience as an independent bookseller, publishing professional, and founder of the Black Swan Salon to illustrate the power of coming together. . . . She illustrates how meaningful conversation can shift a life, deepen a friendship, or plant the seed for a new beginning. And in these trying times, I'm especially appreciative of how Linda-Marie reminds us that when we find the time and place for meaningful connection, we make room for real change."

—MITCHELL KAPLAN, owner of Books & Books

# CREATING A SALON

# CREATING A
## SALON

### THE MAGIC OF CONVERSATIONS THAT MATTER

## LINDA-MARIE BARRETT

A SURREY BOOK
AGATE
CHICAGO

First printed in September 2025

Printed in the United States of America

10 9 8 7 6 5 4 3 2 1            25 26 27 28 29

Library of Congress Cataloging-in-Publication Data
Names: Barrett, Linda-Marie author
Title: Creating a salon : the magic of conversations that matter / Linda-Marie Barrett.
Description: Chicago : Agate Surrey, [2025] | Includes bibliographical references and index. |
Identifiers: LCCN 2025015133 (print) | LCCN 2025015134 (ebook) | ISBN 9781572843561 paperback | ISBN 9781572849006 epub
Subjects: LCSH: Salons | Discussion | Book clubs (Discussion groups)
Classification: LCC LC6519 .B345 2025  (print) | LCC LC6519  (ebook) | DDC 367--dc23/eng/20250526
LC record available at https://lccn.loc.gov/2025015133
LC ebook record available at https://lccn.loc.gov/2025015134

Author photo by Jon Mayes
Cover design by Morgan Krehbiel

Surrey is an imprint of Agate Publishing.
Agate books are available in bulk at discount prices.
For more information, visit agatepublishing.com.

To Jon, my *anam cara*, the most wonderful husband and friend I could ever have imagined. And to all gentle souls seeking to bring more love and support into their communities. This is for you.

**salon (n):** a fashionable assemblage of notables (such as literary figures, artists, or statesmen) held by custom at the home of a prominent person. (Merriam-Webster)

**salon (n):** a cool group of women getting together in a cozy home to share, learn, laugh, and grow. (Annice, Black Swan Salon member)

# Table of Contents

# Bring Community into Your Living Room

"Find a group of people who challenge and inspire you, spend a lot of time with them, and it will change your life."
—Amy Poehler

COMMUNITY IS PRIMAL AND NECESSARY for our mental and physical health. We know this to be true more than ever. In the aftermath of the Covid era, when so many of us isolated for long stretches, we're keenly aware of community's importance to our well-being. Yet, despite the daily connections we make online, in the grocery store, or on familiar walking paths, we rarely experience enough authentic, heart-opening community. We create to-do lists, we calendar professional meetings and deadlines, we may even make a point of regular date nights with our partners, but how often have we put off gatherings with friends and family because we place greater importance on other areas of our lives?

It's not surprising, then, to learn from the U.S. surgeon general's 2023 report *Our Epidemic of Loneliness and Isolation* that our country is experiencing a loneliness epidemic. A key takeaway from the report: "Social connection is as essential to our long-term survival as food and water. But today, loneliness is more widespread than other major health issues in the U.S. Our epidemic of loneliness and isolation is a major public health concern." So many of us yearn for the connectedness we've lost through neglect, changing patterns in how we work, play, and gather, and overreliance on social media as a substitute for community.

In her extraordinary memoir, *H Is for Hawk,* Helen Macdonald realizes her isolation from other people is causing her to sink into a frightening depression. She writes, "'Nature in her green, tranquil woods heals and soothes all affliction.' Now I knew this for what it was: a beguiling but dangerous lie. I was furious with myself and my own conscious certainty that this was the cure I needed. Hands are for other humans to hold. They should not be reserved exclusively as perches for hawks.'"

I remember reading that passage for the first time and being moved to tears because it was my circle of friends and family who helped me through my grieving and rebuilding in the wake of my divorce. I didn't so much reach out my hands as witness hands reaching out to me. I've learned that the best salve for me is not retreating, but being in community, in a shared space, having meaningful conversation; that is the essence of who I am, and how I find peacefulness within myself.

Since 2010, I've hosted a women-only book club called WILD, an acronym for Women in Lively Discussion. We live up to our name, as we spend an animated hour discussing our chosen book and sharing personal stories about the ways the reading resonated with our lives. I get so much from these meetings, but I wanted something more. Years ago I'd been in a salon with women I worked with at a bookstore. Over glasses of wine, we'd talk long into the night about every subject under the sun, nothing off the table, no judgment, and a lot of laughter. One of us once worked at a famous sex-positive adult toy shop in San Francisco, and another grew up in a nudist family featured in a photo spread in a national magazine. There were so many incredible stories! We became close friends for a few magical years, until one by one we drifted apart because of job changes or relocation.

I wanted to experience a salon like that again, where a group could go "off book" and really dig into conversations about important issues like aging, the #MeToo movement, emotional labor, anger, vulnerability, and strength. I looked around at the women in my life—some I knew only a little, others were the best of friends—and intentionally chose women with different passions so we'd represent many viewpoints, not just mirrors of our own. I reached out to a baker, an architect, a composer, a poet, an artist, a writer, a realtor, an interior designer, and a nurse and proposed that we meet to share food and focused discussion. I offered my living room and prepared all the supporting materials. They just needed to show up with a potluck dish, an open mind, and curiosity. And they did. We've been meeting for over eight years now, have gone on retreats and vacationed together in Canada. What we've created is beautiful and sustaining. We are friends for life, safe harbors if we need them, a circle of love.

I invite you to create the same kind of community in your life because real connection is what we all need right now. Whether you seek to enhance the gatherings you already arrange or attend, or hope to create something altogether new, hosting salons will be a life-changing experience. In this book, I'll give you the tools to get started, become a confident facilitator, and bring community into your living room.

# LET'S BEGIN

# WHY I HOST SALONS

"Hope begins in the dark. The stubborn hope that if you just show up and try to do the right thing, the dawn will come. You wait and watch and work: you don't give up."

—ANNE LAMOTT

HOSTING SALONS IS A POWERFUL way to create an intentional community that deepens and broadens a circle of friends; salons can provide the support we all need during life's inevitable challenges, and inspiration when we're in those threshold moments of creative imagining. But, in keeping with the saying "When the student is ready, the teacher will appear," it was an issue of timing for me. I was ready to take on hosting salons only after I'd made important changes in my personal and professional life. Salons turned out to be a reward, in a sense, for all the work I'd done in my midlife journey to take back my dreams.

\*\*\*

"Don't make yourself small to make someone else comfortable." A friend offered this advice before I attended an event where I would be seeing someone who was not keen on seeing me. We'd never met, but she quite unwaveringly associated me with past hurt and had told others that I was in the "we'll never be friends" category. My friend's words rang in my head when I was left alone with this person while others were busy rehearsing an element of the gathering. We had to wait for their return, so leaving was not an option. We stood in silence, not facing each other. I didn't make the situation easier, as I would have done earlier in life, by offering up some blithe commentary or a joke to cut the tension. I didn't make myself small. I took a breath, stretched my spine to stand a bit taller, and held my silence. She finally spoke. Or broke, I'm not sure which, but we exchanged pleasantries about the weather. And that was it.

I've made myself small a lot of my life, to appease others who had volatile personalities, who were easily wounded and could turn on me, who made it clear that their needs were more important than mine. And by making myself small, I hurt my spirit. I was once a very cocky, almost fearless kid, who ran at life with arms wide open. Everything I touched seemed to turn to gold. I was athletic and musical, a storyteller, poet, chanteuse (or so I imagined when I performed Carpenters songs for my friends), and an elementary school orator. But at some point, as a sensitive child with parents overwhelmed by financial and personal struggles, I got quieter. I still put myself out there, but that expansive me? That me shrank.

I was one of five children, squarely in the middle, and felt early on very different from my family (Did they have inner lives? Could we not talk about what was going on?). Epic fights between siblings, unacknowledged alcoholism, financial instability, and an insistence on observing religious and dietary rules that caused me anguish rendered our home an emotional minefield, at least for me. I even put a padlock on my bedroom door, which my parents allowed but didn't comment on, to create a personal safety zone. As a fan of books about fairy tales and magic, I believed I was a changeling and held on to that notion for a long time. I now understand we were all doing the best we could in trying circumstances, but instead of banding together, it felt like everybody was looking out for themselves.

I applied to colleges on my own, reading through the promotional postcards and brochures that arrived at our house to lure this resident high school senior to attend. I selected a few that appealed to me because of their programming, prestige, and location (far enough away that I would live there). I went to the one that offered the biggest scholarship, a decision my parents heartily endorsed. I was academically successful but began to collapse under the strain of caring for myself.

I was in a perpetual panic about my future, which worsened as graduation loomed. This bled into my relationship with my boyfriend, who was deeply loving but, like me, conflict avoidant to a fault, and our relationship imploded after senior year. In my grief over losing him, and feeling very alone in the world, I made a strikingly poor decision to abandon a graduate fellowship at Cornell and move across country to live with someone I barely knew. Like so many young women, I put a romanticized notion of being loved above the work of loving myself, and I foundered.

My twenties through forties were often very difficult, but when I look back, I try to find gold in the darkness. All the moments of our lives form a kind of tapestry; they are parts of the fabric of who we are, and it's important for me, when I question the value and impact of my life's passage, to occasionally sift within the ugliness to find those shiny pieces of experience, the gold threads, that brought a smile, a deep sense of peace, a connection with the cosmic goodness that's always out there for us. During those years, I did many things that brought me great pleasure, among them every form of homesteading on a picturesque farm in the mountains. I cradled newborn lambs and helped them get their first drink of milk, pressed apples from our orchard to make sparkling wine, spun wool from our sheep on my Ashford spinning wheel, walked in the woods during summer nights, my way lit by the flickering light of fireflies. Many a summer afternoon I lay on my back in the fields behind our farmhouse to watch hawks circle above in the blue, blue skies.

I reclaimed control over my life at forty-eight, having so constrained myself in dysfunctional relationships that I risked becoming a shadow. A decade earlier I was asked by a friend what my dreams were, and I told her I had no dreams. I vividly recall that conversation. I didn't even feel the sadness that should have come with a statement like that, but rather a resigned numbness. I'd experienced trauma that caused me to shake so hard my teeth chattered, times when I took drops of valerian and kava kava just to get through a workday. But I soldiered on for another ten years until I could no longer ignore the truth—that the path I was on was killing me. It was essential to let go, start over, and rebuild.

I began to do a lot of discerning around my friend relationships. My therapist, who gracefully guided me through my divorce, often pushed me to consider why certain people were in my life, whether they were showing themselves to be supportive through their actions. She would even bluntly interrupt me, almost a dart to the heart, and say, "That person is NOT your friend." It's a very hard thing to realize that someone you thought was your friend is not, that they hold certain beliefs about you that you cannot overcome, or that you are serving some purpose for them that is more utilitarian than heartfelt. To honor the life I was creating, I winnowed down my circle of friends to just a few beloveds. In the years that have passed since this time, life has been so much sweeter and free of needless drama. Careful friend-pruning can make your inner tree bloom much more brightly!

We hear so much about the word *curation* these days. As overused as it sometimes is, it perfectly describes how I assembled my post-forty-eight life. I looked at each element and questioned it in a way inspired by Marie Kondo's *The Life-Changing Magic of Tidying Up*: Does this bring me joy? Most of my life then did not give me joy. It was hard as hell. Divorce depleted me financially, and I watched as long-aspired-to plans fell away like a house of cards in the aftermath. I lived alone, no TV, no microwave, hardly any furniture. I was not sleeping well due to a perfect storm of perimenopause and untreated PTSD. I struggled to keep weight on, and my hair was falling out from stress. I avoided mirrors. But, with the help of supportive loved ones, I got through it. I built a new friend circle, fell in love with my now husband, and started eye movement desensitization and reprocessing (EMDR) therapy. I left a long-term job for one that offered a different set of challenges and a new group of folks to work with. And I began to write and play my flute again, to cook, dance, and laugh. I'd made a fresh start at midlife.

So we come at last to why I host salons. Hosting a salon turned out to be a pivotal step in my journey to stop being small and to stretch my wings. At different points in my life I've experienced moments when the air shifts and I step outside of myself. I become witness, observing as if I were looking through two cameras: one pulling back from the scene, recording, the other traveling behind my eyes, down into my center, like an endoscope viewing my internal responses. Becoming witness can be an act of self-preservation, to cast up a sanctuarial boundary when what is happening is too disturbing, even dangerous, to be directly exposed to.

But it can also occur when I realize something very special and beautiful is taking place, whether a moment when the hard work of personal stewardship has paid off, or just the extraordinary luck to be present for something that feels miraculous. We tend to remember the bad more often than the good, as part of our survival instinct, but these happy times wash over me like the warm, salty water of the sea, buoying and healing me. Such a moment happened during one of our first salons, "Birthing a Dream & Letting Something Go." We'd been together for a year, this was our third salon, and I was still getting to know some of the members. The salon's theme reflected how far I'd come, from the woman who'd despaired of having dreams, to someone who now dared to pursue one. I was hopeful entering this salon, believing the dream I was going to birth, this tender little bird in the palm of my hand, had a good chance of actually taking wing.

At the salon itself, we gathered in small groups and spoke our dreams aloud, to make ourselves accountable to them and gather feedback. For most salon members, the dream called for a specific action—starting or closing a business, ending a relationship, submitting a writing project, a bucket-list trip, a fitness journey.

As we talked, and laughed, and wrote down our dreams on cards that I would later mail to them, I felt that shift of becoming witness. I looked around and saw us leaning in toward each other, offering words of support, studiously taking in someone else's plan. Gentle smiles, little pats on the hand or shoulder, laughter, clapping hands, nervousness replaced by joy. My heart expanded and softened, unfurling like a flower. I realized that in the few years since I'd started over, I'd created so much positive change, strikingly apparent in the salon before me. When you're making big changes you have no idea what's going to happen. You just know you need to change, that the struggle of holding on is worse than letting go, and you guard like a precious thing your faith that up ahead, although you can't see it yet, and might not even be able to imagine it yet, is a new life, one you'll have more power shaping into what you want it to be. Step by step, loosening my grip on the past and reaching for the dreams I knew in my heart were still available to me, I'd created this new life. As if a hand pulled back a curtain to reveal the soft light of a sky after a rain, the sun casting a rainbow against a backdrop of fading storm clouds, I could see the beauty of this shining new life before me. The women in my salon were there for each other. We'd formed a team to fulfill the mission set out for our salon: *to inspire, encourage, and support each other in our creative pursuits and life dreams.* We had each other's backs. And that, in my world, is everything.

Hosting a salon didn't require me to be an extrovert or have the hosting skills of Martha Stewart because if it did, I wouldn't be writing this book. I'm not always the smoothest socially. I can be shy and a bit awkward; I might interrupt at the wrong times, or stay silent when I could instead slip into the conversation. I scan a lot, too, a remnant of my "child of an alcoholic" legacy. I'd been an event planner professionally for many years, but this kind of gathering was much more intimate. Outside of hosting a book club, the events I worked on for our bookstore always centered someone else, usually an author. When you host a salon, your presence is central, which can be uncomfortable if you prefer the sidelines. Yet I soon discovered that putting together events where friendships can take root and blossom is an area where I have a lot of passion, and any personal risk or vulnerability on my part is well worth it. Despite all the ways I could pick myself apart (see above), I turned out to be a great salon host. The experience has enriched my life beyond my wildest expectations. I want the same for you.

For those who wish to find their voice, or raise their voice, and encourage others to do the same, I urge you to start a salon, or accept an invitation to attend one. Trust me, it's not about being the perfect host or guest, or knowing everything, or anything, on the subject. Salons are places where you can show up as yourself and engage to the level you feel comfortable. However your life has led you to this moment, you can take a breath, stretch your spine, and be part of a community of seekers and sharers who just might transform your life.

# WHAT'S YOUR MOTIVATION?

"And the time came when the risk to remain tight in a bud was
more painful than the risk it took to blossom."
—ANAÏS NIN

STARTING A SALON IS A big step. Before you set things in
motion, think about what personally motivates you to dedicate time and energy to building a new community. I've done
some introspection on motivation around the book club I host
monthly. It's a considerable commitment in time: organizing
and vetting the book selection for the year, managing email
messaging and follow-up communications with members, giving the bookstore we're affiliated with a heads up so they can
order in the books, reading the books each month, thinking
about how to run the meetings, showing up at the venue and
reserving space. Then there are the intangibles, like how the
month's reading choice becomes my bedtime reading, which
isn't always a good match and can affect my sleep.

Some days hosting the book club feels like a burden. Like
when the book choice turns out to be one I'm not crazy about,
or I'm tired from a long day at work and the idea of driving
downtown to lead a book discussion isn't all that appealing. If I
were not the host, I could take the night off, but as host, others
are depending on me, and I don't want to let them down. So,
I ponder my motivations from time to time to remind myself
why I'm doing this. My main motivations are to foster community around reading and to discuss books that explore different ways of moving and being in the world; in our club's case,

books from a woman (cis or trans) or non-binary author's perspective. These are deep passions of mine, and my life's work as a bookseller and executive director of a trade organization for independent bookstores.

Priceless benefits of the book club are meeting people who become friends outside of our meetings and hearing other views and insights on what we're reading. I give my time and talents around book selection and discussion, and I get back so much from being part of a fun group of women with similar interests.

When you consider starting a salon, think about how it connects with one or more of your passions; how you feed yourself on this journey will sustain you when the salon gets challenging, and it likely will. You'll recall your motivations when you need affirmation that "this is why I'm hosting a salon."

I decided to create a salon when I was initiating a lot of personal changes. I was recently divorced and about to shift career paths, leaving a job and workplace I'd devoted myself to since graduate school. To make these changes happen, I had to prompt difficult conversations with people who didn't approve of the decisions I was making. If you've been there, you know such times can be grueling and take a lot of strength and patience to work through while staying true to your goals.

It was during this period of shedding and rebuilding that I came up with the idea of starting a salon. I didn't want to be isolated; I was ready to step fully into life again. I drew up a short list of motivations: Create a space for deep discussions of ideas, make new friends, host potlucks, and foster community among my guests.

I was also moved to think about whether my personal motivations complemented my main goal for the salon: *to inspire, encourage, and support each other in our creative pursuits and life dreams.* This is a critical conversation to have with yourself. Take out a piece of paper and write "Personal Motivations" at the top left, then list whatever comes into your head (you can always edit later). Then write "Salon Goals" on the top right and list any goals you hope to accomplish at your salon. Do your motivations support the goals of the salon? If you made a Venn diagram of your personal motivations and your salon goals, would there be a center (ideally, heart-shaped) where the two lists converge? As you're inviting others to be part of something that serves the group in some larger way, it can't be "all about me." For people to set aside precious time in their lives for a salon, it has to be very meaningful to them as well. I'll show you how I worked through my personal motivations in the context of my salon goals to make sure I was fulfilling both with my approach.

Perhaps the first motivation, creating a space for a deep discussion of ideas, which is the raison d'être for most salons, is the least obvious to connect to how the salon supports each of us individually in our creative pursuits and life dreams. How does attending a salon on aging, for example, help someone working on an art project or starting a business achieve their goals? It helps because putting yourself, especially a receptive you, into gatherings like salons is a proven way to nurture your creative aspirations.

I've always loved long rambling conversations over a glass of wine or mug of tea, candles lit, soft music in the background. Pick a topic, and let's share what we know about it, our feelings, too, and how it might touch upon our lives. Setting my mind to a subject and teasing out elements to ponder stirs up my creativity on a deep level and often clarifies my thoughts in seemingly unrelated areas. Steven Benbow, the founder and chief writer of Awkward Silence, a conversation-starter business, discusses in his article "20 Benefits of Conversation" the way conversation helps us bond and "sparks ideas [and] creates synergy: Conversations are the mixing bowls that great ideas emerge from." Engaging with others in artful conversation helps us to better know who we are and what we are capable of.

I remember listening to Steven Johnson, author of *How We Got to Now: Six Innovations That Made the Modern World*, present at the American Booksellers Association's Winter Institute in Asheville, North Carolina, in 2015. He shared how throughout history folks have gathered in "third places," places other than the home (the first place) and work-place (the second place), to discuss ideas, sometimes resulting in history-changing innovations. Coffee houses, independent bookstores, and, certainly, salons are such third places. He elaborates on this concept in *Where Good Ideas Come From: The Natural History of Innovation*, emphasizing how innovation comes from social interaction. It's not always a straight line of thought or a shining eureka moment that leads to a creative breakthrough. It can be the result of conversations on unrelated subjects that spark a wholly different approach to something you're thinking about, involved in shaping, or in the process of working through.

An example of this happened in a yoga class. My teacher, who often gifted us with snippets of wisdom wrapped in everyday anecdotes, shared that one of her students decided to reverse the order of how she did things in her shower. Her new routine started with brushing her teeth, then shampooing and conditioning her hair, and then soaping her body, instead of her usual approach. From this one pattern shift in her life, she reported that *everything* changed, including looking anew at her professional work and bravely switching careers, and selling her home to downsize to a condo. We were encouraged in this class to not always put our mat in the same place in the room, but to be intentionally random about it. These examples of breaking routines became a challenge for me and inspired me to make other changes, which led to other changes, none of which had to do with showering or yoga classes. You get the picture! In our discussions in the salon, we give room for little nudges, float tiny possibilities, which just might become something big for someone in the room, in an area of their life that has nothing to do, on the surface, with the subject we're exploring. The salons become both sounding board and springboard for personal innovation. Members have shared that they've been inspired by our gatherings to create paintings, write poetry, compose a piece of music, even make career or big personal relationship changes. When I envision the salon in action, I imagine our brains sparking joyfully, our souls smiling, and positive energy swirling in the air between us. This vision motivates me every time we meet.

Making new friends, or deepening existing friendships, is one of the best reasons to host or attend salons. We often don't make time for deep conversations on subjects outside of a current crisis, and conversation is one of the most important ways we can really see and understand each other—where, if we feel safe and brave enough, we can remove the filters and cloaks we wrap ourselves in to make daily life easier, and be our truest selves. We might even become soul friends if we are so fortunate in our salon mates, forming deep and lasting bonds.

How does making new friends align with the salon's goals to inspire, encourage, and support each other in our creative pursuits and life dreams? After the "friend-pruning" I initiated during the first years of my personal reinvention, I really only had a few confidantes. I hoped to expand my circle of friends when I carefully selected members for the salon. Each exemplified kindness and intellectual curiosity, which was affirmed when they accepted the invitation to join the salon! They also weren't from the parts of my life I was trying to change, so they had no stake in me being a certain way. I could work on myself in their presence, try out new ways of being me, and they could do the same. An important piece of advice I've taken to heart was echoed by author Mel Robbins. It's on the topic of whom you surround yourself with when you're making life changes. I'm paraphrasing from her Instagram feed (I find my inspiration everywhere, truly): "When making changes, look to those who have made the changes. Existing friends helped enable the life you led, and often don't like the decisions you are making, and might talk you out of them. Look to mentors, to folks who have done the work." The women I invited were clearly doing the work; I knew from my limited interactions with them, and from their reputations in our community, that they were generous, good-hearted people who'd mentored others.

From our first meeting, buoyed by our salon's safe and supportive space, conversation naturally drifted to personal and professional work that related to the theme in some way.

Because we came from different career paths, there was no competition, and instead we could offer each other refreshing outsider perspectives on ideas we were playing with. Over time, folks stepped in regularly to lend their skills to another member looking to try something new and in need of support. At a recent salon, a retired professor offered to help a writer draft a syllabus for an online teaching opportunity, and an architect advised another member on flooring choices for her kitchen. Many members have become friends outside of the salon, with a few of us starting a therapeutic support group that now meets weekly online. We're all committed to each other's success, however we define it.

Lastly, do potluck socials help us in our creative pursuits and life dreams? A resounding hell yes! I'm a big fan of potluck socials. They're an easy and informal way to fill a table with food and are very communal and inclusive, as each person brings a dish that reflects a personal choice and even eating preferences. Whether they purchased something or cooked it at home, they spent some time thinking about what they'd bring, which connects them to the greater salon experience. Offering folks a range of choices—to bring an appetizer, a dessert, or something that's more of a main dish—also brings latitude and creativity into the process. Every potluck is a surprise party! Sharing food is also a timeless way to create connection, and perhaps one of the most personal. We've touched this food, sometimes we chose certain items in the store with the dish in mind, then combined them to make a delicious offering, using a special plate or bowl that enhances the presentation. Or we may have gone to the hot bar in a grocery store and selected a few items that arrive in a to-go container that we replate more attractively and warm up in the host's microwave. In any case, a potluck encourages thoughtfulness, generosity, advance planning, and connection, feeding us in so many ways to support our individual journeys. Jennie Allen, in her inspiring book *Find Your People: Building Deep Community in a Lonely World* reminds us what we all intuitively know: "Throughout history and cultures, coming to a table, breaking bread together, has always represented reconciliation and healing. In all my travels and conversations about the topic of community, this has come up again and again. From Italy to Africa, food. Meals. Tables. People consistently and regularly come together around food."

(Note: If potlucks are not your thing, you can change it up by meeting in different restaurants or cafés, catering in food to your home, or eliminating food from the program. Nothing wrong with a bowl of mini candy bars or M&M's.)

Once you've identified your motivations, you can begin thinking further about defining the goals for your salon and perhaps even creating a special identity or name for it. We'll explore how to do that and more in our next chapter, and look at other elements of the salon such as setting and timing, choosing the folks you'd like to invite, and creating ground rules. Let's get started!

# ELEMENTS OF A SUCCESSFUL SALON

"Face-to-face conversation is the most human—and humanizing—
thing we do. Fully present to one another, we learn to listen. It's
where we develop the capacity for empathy. It's where we experience the joy of being heard, of being understood."
—SHERRY TURKLE, *Reclaiming Conversation: The Power of Talk in
a Digital Age*

SALONS HAVE CULTURAL ROOTS ACROSS the planet, with
salon-like gatherings reported in every part of the world,
in marketplaces and coffeehouses, literary clubs and drawing
rooms, in temples and walled gardens. Salons are spaces that
center conversation and the discussion of ideas; they're associated with innovation, artistic experimentation, and political
movements. Because they've most often been run and attended
by women, salons have also provided education, and a voice
in important cultural movements, to women otherwise denied
these opportunities; in this way, they have also contributed to
social reform. From my vantage point, what's not to love?

The origin of the word *salon* is French, and means the room
where guests are received, a reception or drawing room, a par-
lor. It's a noteworthy example of naming gatherings after the
rooms they are hosted in, the way cabinet, the word for a private room or study in the homes of nobility, took on the additional meaning of meetings for councils and advisors. The first
salons in France—the kinds of salons many of us think of when
we envision them—are traced to the early 1600s and grew in
popularity during the Enlightenment. They were usually hosted
at the homes of prominent people and led by a woman host,
called a *salonnière*, who invited guests, planned the meals and
entertainment, and directed conversation. Salon culture spread

across Europe, springing up in Vienna, London, Dublin, and then in Boston, New York City, Washington, D.C., and further west, continuing to this day.

Salons are sometimes associated with intellectual elitism because the most famous salons took place at the homes of wealthy women with high social status who invited their wealthy friends. But they've also long functioned as places to workshop new forms of music, literature, art, and philosophy before a small audience. They've been frequented by people with different interests and passions—scientists, inventors, artists, writers, actors, philosophers, composers—representing a mix of economic classes and religious and secular backgrounds, all of which encourages lively atmospheres for debate and inspiration. They're more structured and focused than an informal hangout or casual dinner party, but they can be whatever you want them to be. Some modern salons host multiple layers of experience within their gatherings, serving as a place for discussion, a listening room for live music, and a platform for poetry readings.

When I thought about the kind of salon I wanted to host, my mind went to the salons of Gertrude Stein and Alice B. Toklas in Paris, as well as those of the Bloomsbury Group, outside of London, both held in the early twentieth century. Unlike theirs, mine would be women-only, but we would be similarly wide-ranging in our discussions and represent many backgrounds and interests. Could we have a Picasso or Virginia Woolf among us, as theirs did? Perhaps, but most important to me was to provide a space and opportunity to engage in deep and meaningful conversations, to foster community and really connect, person to person. I built my salon with those intentions and am sharing in this chapter some important details and considerations to bear in mind as you start your own. These tips are a great starting point if you're new to hosting salons, though you may adjust here and there, as suits your personality, circumstances, and purposes.

Successful salons include the following elements: consistent setting and timing, defined goals and identity, people who mesh well and respect each other, and ground rules that are shared and followed. There are two more elements that are often neglected, but absolutely essential: structure and an attentive host. I'll speak to these first.

## STRUCTURE AND AN ATTENTIVE HOST

I've found that a combination of loose structure and gentle direction—or what Priya Parker, author of every host's must-read, *The Art of Gathering*, calls generous authority, "imposing in a way that serves your guests"—makes for a successful and memorable salon. We often attend informal parties without a clear beginning or end, a mix and mingle without hostly direction. This kind of scenario can be fun to attend. A casual gathering offers a "choose your own adventure" path where every part of the journey is up to you. You get to decide when to arrive, how much you want to participate, whom to speak to, whom to sit next to, and when to leave. When the stakes are low for what you hope to get out of going to the event in the first place (maybe you just want to catch up with some folks you rarely see, or to see the inside of the host's home, which you've always been curious about), unstructured is good! Sometimes that kind of gathering is just what your mood and emotional energy require.

When you host a salon, however, structure and direction are essential for it going according to plan; your guests are freed from scanning for clues as to what to do when, and can focus on the main reason for a salon gathering: deep discussion. You'll need to step up and be an attentive and engaged host, to shepherd things along without being heavy-handed. This admittedly can be uncomfortable at times, especially if you're on the introverted side. I still get a bit of nerves when I host a salon, and I've been hosting them for years. We're human, things go wrong, people sometimes resist being directed, and it takes courage in the face of risk, particularly when you're hosting the first of what you hope will be a series of meetings. I hate interrupting folks while they're talking, especially when it's obvious they're enjoying themselves. However, right from the beginning of hosting salons I realized I had to be assertive if I ever wanted us to move along from the initial catch-up to eating the food we'd brought for the potluck. My salon members love to share with each other, and some only see each other at these gatherings, which I host quarterly. If I didn't wedge myself into their conversations (sometimes even physically pushing into the space between two folks talking, which feels super awkward, but I try to make it gentle and funny at the same time) and signal it's time to move on, we might be catching up for the entire salon.

If you're nice about it, not barking orders but instead kindly instructing folks that it's time to transition to the next stage of the gathering, you won't spark a rebellion, unless your guests are already inclined in that direction (and I would hope they're not). Think about those times when you've attended events and noticed the host initiating sitting down for the meal, offering a blessing or calling for a toast, ushering folks into the living room, bringing out a board game, taking a group photo, etc. Especially if you're always leading in your professional life, isn't there something deeply relaxing about being led by a host who has a plan for the event? Be that kind of salon host, or at least aim to be. And if this sounds intimidating, consider bringing in a cohost to help direct salon flow. You don't have to do it all.

### SETTING AND TIMING

When you decide to start a salon, consider what you want to accomplish during the group's time together and how the setting and timing will help make that happen. We'll look at setting in more detail in the chapter "Making the Experience Richer," but for now, let's consider the basics: Will this be an online or in-person salon? If in-person, do you want to meet in someone's home or at a neutral venue, like a meeting space in a hotel, community center, business, or local bookstore? If the weather is reliably pleasant, would you like to try an outside setting, perhaps in a nearby park that has a gazebo and will accommodate members bringing folding camp chairs? Would you like your salon to include food, which could make a café or restaurant more appealing? Will your setting allow for privacy, especially if you're discussing personal subjects?

My book club, for instance, used to meet in the bookstore. Although being surrounded by books sounds like a perfect background for discussing them, there were a number of negatives that affected our time together. The chairs were hard and uncomfortable, we couldn't bring drinks into the area where we met, and the location of the meeting area within the bookstore was particularly inappropriate for our group. At that time, our book club discussed romances, and we were meeting in the children's section. I remember us leaning in toward each other as we whispered our thoughts about *Fifty Shades of Grey*. We had to be extra careful in how we expressed ourselves because of children browsing nearby. No bawdy jokes or allusions to particular sexual acts and positions allowed! After the *Fifty Shades* meeting debacle, we decided to switch to a venue that felt more like an adult night out, with comfy seating, drinks, and food options. We now gather at a rooftop bar downtown. It's centrally located to our members, needs no reservations, has parking on the ground floor, and offers food, cocktails, and nonalcoholic drinks. The seating is super comfy and the views of downtown and surrounding mountains are always breathtaking! Only adults wander by, and the atmosphere is lively, so our conversation, should it need to be more private, is less likely to be overheard. The venue meets all our needs. It wouldn't work for the salon, though, as it doesn't offer enough privacy for the very personal discussions we have.

For my salon, I decided we would meet at my home. This is a more traditional setting for salons, which over the centuries have been hosted in private homes around the world. Hosting in my home gives me more control over the environment, an element I like to tweak for each gathering. And it's my comfort zone, where I can host with confidence. I have enough space in my living room for everyone, and additional rooms for when we break up into smaller group discussions. Parking is plentiful on the street outside, and the setup is very accessible for those with mobility issues.

Regarding timing, will yours be a morning, afternoon, or evening gathering? How often do you want to meet? Weekly, monthly, quarterly? Maybe you won't know the answers to these questions at first, or you'll need to pivot based on feedback from your salon, but think about them as you set things up and see where they lead you. You might poll a few friends who have hosted similar gatherings to find out what works for them.

To fit into my busy schedule, and not feel like a huge commitment or burden to me or attendees, I decided our salon would meet quarterly. We meet on a weekday evening, to reduce potential conflicts with work and family schedules, and we begin at five p.m., an early start especially appreciated in winter, when the days are short and night driving sometimes includes navigating icy roads. For the meetings themselves, I've structured them as follows: The salons last for two and a half hours. We share a vegetarian potluck before our discussion, allotting forty-five minutes to an hour for the casual meal. After we eat and catch up, I signal it's time for discussion. I usually begin with a brief introduction to the topic and my personal take on it. Then I may (depending on the theme) pass around clipboards bearing a questionnaire I've created that invites members to reflect on a number of topic-related questions. Filling out the questionnaire brings the energy down to support focus and provides a document members can take home after the salon to think more on or stow in their journals as a memento. After ten minutes, we move into small breakouts for about fifteen minutes, and then into a general discussion. If you're meeting online, you can follow a similar format and do small breakout rooms on platforms like Zoom. During the general discussion, I pose a question, and one by one, round-robin style, we answer, with a bit of room for back-and-forth response, member to member. When we come to the final ten minutes, we read aloud quotations by notable people (artists, philosophers, scientists, etc.) provided by members that relate to the evening's topic, and then do a formal closing of our time together. The salon begins at five, discussion by six, and close at seven thirty, though members are invited to linger. We recently added a clothing swap at the end, so the gatherings go on longer, but at that point staying is optional. My husband is away or in a back room of the house while we meet, giving us privacy for a women-only gathering. This means a lot to our members.

I've played around with the length of the salon, shortening it to two hours on occasion, but because we include a meal and social time, I've found that two hours is just not long enough to get to each part of the program without a level of sacrifice and rush. Members are quite familiar with the 2.5-hour format, too, and expect things to follow a certain path (they don't even groan when I bring out the clipboards). They've become easier to usher along to each stage and encourage any newbies to follow along. As the salon is quarterly, it can bear being what some might otherwise view as "long," but it really never feels that way to us.

## DEFINED GOALS AND IDENTITY

It's important to think about your goals for this salon and be clear with potential members what those are, so they can consider how they align with them before accepting your invitation. Do you seek to bridge differences through dialogue? To explore issues affecting your community? To dive deeper into literary discussion than a book club allows? To examine themes central to the makeup—age, gender, race, profession, economic class, religious identity, etc.—of your membership? Envision what you hope your members will get out of salon gatherings, and then define it, as if crafting a kind of mission statement. You might even give your salon a name, or identity, to elevate it to an extra level of specialness. I worked on fleshing out my salon's goals and identity with the help of two close friends who also became the original salon members. Their feedback helped me clarify what I wanted to do with the salon and how best to present that information through my invitation.

I knew I wanted us to be women-only. I've spent most of my life in men's headspaces, through required reading at every level of my education, through media in every form, and at gatherings that include men, who tend to dominate conversations. I yearned for female perspectives in female-only spaces. I named our salon the Black Swan Salon because of the symbolism of black swans, which are considered a surprise and representative of big changes. I thought of our group of women as powerful, surely with power we didn't even realize ourselves, but which would become visible and manifest through the work we did together and our mutual support to live our best lives. This was how I defined our salon:

> Black Swan events are rare, unpredictable, and often life-changing. Black swans symbolize mystery, creativity, and insight. They are beautiful and strong, and when they are vulnerable, they work together as a group to protect each other. Join this gathering of women to eat, drink, be merry, and look to the future. Our goal is to inspire, encourage, and support each other in our creative pursuits and life dreams.

Members of my salon began to identify as Black Swans. I created a Facebook group for us to announce our gatherings, share articles we loved, and talk about what was going on in our lives between meetings. I drew a metaphorical circle around us to define us, and set the stage for bonding as a group.

## INVITING PEOPLE WHO MESH WELL

This is tricky and worth much thought. One of the greatest challenges for a salon host is facilitating a discussion in which every voice is heard, and no one person hogs the stage. You are the conductor of the orchestra you seek to create. Think of people who will be in harmony and engage in a way that supports a beautifully resonant overtone. Do you want to bring in a diva? Or someone who shrinks from participating? Probably not at first, until you feel confident about leading and eliciting respectful, engaging, and enlightening conversation among potentially challenging personalities. I recommend starting small. I didn't think everyone I invited to my first salon would accept and I wound up with too many people, though this situation resolved after a few meetings. If I could do it again, I would start with a group of five or six members, folks you know from experience will not grab hold of the discussion for their own purposes.

First, consider the friends you already have. Would any of them be interested in meeting salon-style to discuss topics? If you have to pick and choose among friends, could that cause a rift? We have friends for different reasons and perhaps some of them are less inclined to sit for two hours and talk, or they aren't keen on being led by someone else; they chafe against structure. You might be adventurous and invite people you don't know but want to know better, and also be a matchmaker, bringing in folks who don't know each other but whom you suspect will very much like each other. I was adventuress and matchmaker, inviting women I wanted to know better and whom I thought would really appreciate the other members. I also chose women representing a variety of professions, married and unmarried, mothers and childfree. Our ages ranged from mid-forties to mid-eighties. I purposely chose these forms of diversity, and it has worked out well, no culling required. When the group loses a member because they move away or have other pressing commitments, I *very* thoughtfully bring in new folks one at a time. We have a great vibe going on now and I don't want to mess with it.

### RULES OF ENGAGEMENT (AKA GROUND RULES)

Setting up ground rules is crucial and, once explained and understood, allows the group more ease with discussion. In their delightful book, *Friendshipping: The Art of Finding Friends, Being Friends, and Keeping Friends*, authors Jenn Bane and Trin Garritano offer great tips in their chapter "How to Host a Group Hangout," including this one: "Setting extremely clear expectations, for any event, is a real courtesy." As host and as an attendee at other events, I completely agree. You can never go wrong with bringing clarity to expectations.

Here are some rules I established before our first gathering, gleaned from doing research on best practices for similar groups. Feel free to use these:

> We each share the responsibility for making this group work.
> We accept people as they are, and avoid making judgments.
> Everyone is given an opportunity to share.
> We have the right to speak and the right to remain silent.
> We give supportive attention to the person who is speaking and don't have side conversations.
> We avoid interrupting.
> We have the right to ask questions and the right to refuse to answer.
> We begin and end our meetings on time.
> We respect confidentiality and don't share what is discussed outside of the salon, even with our partners.

Other rules could be not giving advice unless requested (this is very important in our salon; we are not there to try and fix each other) and not dwelling on unrelated long-past experiences that might be more suited for a moderated therapeutic gathering. Sometimes, because of the subject matter, the topic strays, but as an engaged host, you're there to make sure it comes back to the theme.

Now that you've worked through the basic elements of a salon, it's time to fine-tune your approach to make your salon shine. In the next section we'll look at salon flow, discussion styles, troubleshooting what can go wrong, enriching the experience, and creating your first salon from beginning to end.

# FINE-TUNING

# Beginnings and Endings

"I think of gatherings as a temporary alternative world, with a beginning, a middle, and an end."

—PRIYA PARKER, *The Art of Gathering*

How you begin and end events is critical: One sets the tone for the gathering, the other casts a final impression on the experience. As a host who has learned the hard way—don't neglect either. I'm a believer in the wise saying by Benjamin Franklin, "An ounce of prevention is worth a pound of cure." Creating a plan for the beginnings and endings of your events will go a long way toward ensuring success and avoiding problems you'll have to make up for in the moment.

## BEGINNINGS

When we visit people's homes or other intimate settings, we're usually greeted by the host; we take off our coats, walk into a room full of people, and put down the dish we've brought onto the food table before scanning for the bar. This transition can feel rushed, chaotic, a somewhat jarring whoosh of energy after a quiet drive or walk over. Or it can be smooth and convivial, a settling in with friends, and strangers who may become friends. The entry sets a tone for the evening. What tone would you like to set?

For my salon, I want folks to relax into a welcoming, beautiful space. From my experience, the more comfortable and cared for we feel in a setting, the fewer potential obstacles in the way of settling in, and the more likely we can open our hearts and speak from a place of curiosity and honesty.

I set the stage by arranging seating ahead of time, dimming the lighting to a soft glow, diffusing an uplifting scent (lavender, lime, and grapefruit essential oils are a perfect blend for this mood), prepping the food table with serving utensils, trivets, napkins, and a vase of flowers. I set up the bar with a pitcher of water infused with cucumbers and strawberries or oranges, and I open a few bottles of red and white wine, with glasses and napkins nearby. Coffee and tea are on hand, if anyone wants something hot. By taking time to make sure our meeting area is ready, none of us needs to look for something that might be missing. We can focus instead on each other and the welcoming.

The energy runs high as folks arrive for my salons, and this is true virtually and in person. As host, I choose to let this energy disperse naturally, rather than usher it out quickly; folks want to greet each other, catch up, and begin to bond as a group again. It's a flurry of hugs and then a kind of dance as we place our potluck offerings on the table and get something to drink from the bar. During this time I often step back and catch myself smiling at how we've all clustered together in one spot, almost a huddle. It's a joyful moment to witness. After a certain point, maybe ten to fifteen minutes in, I'll gently nudge folks to begin eating, or if virtual, to start discussion of the salon's topic. Sometimes I feel like a shepherd wielding my shepherd's crook to steer salon members toward the food table or living room. With a smile and determination, and sometimes repeated nudging and waving my hand like a game show host in the direction I want folks to move, I get it done.

### OTHER WAYS TO MAKE BEGINNINGS EASIER:

> If the weather is cold or wet, you'll need to accommodate more space for coats in the front closet or on a bed. Clear out most of your coats from the front closet to free up hangers, or prepare the room where extra coats might go, if that's the alternative. Consider a place or stand for umbrellas, and make sure that you have good lighting in the entranceway and around any steps.

> If you're a "no shoes" household, communicate this in advance so folks will wear comfy socks or bring "inside shoes." Some folks need to wear shoes because of balance or issues with their feet, and others would probably amend their wardrobe choices if they know it's a shoes-off situation. Having to figure out how to deal with your rules on the spot is not a great beginning to any event. Make sure that the entryway where folks take off their shoes has seating and a place to stow shoes so they don't pile up and get in the way of more folks coming in. Beware of tripping hazards.

> Reserve a space for yourself among the seats, a spot where you can easily see everyone and guide discussion. I print out a "reserved for host" sign and place it on my chair to make this happen without a fuss. I failed to do this once and it affected everything. I had to crane my neck to see a few members, making it hard to direct conversation. I was no longer in the largest chair, which adds a level of authority when you're hosting (I think of it as a feng shui power position), and, for me, that's important.

> Place any salon materials (clipboards, questionnaires, quotes to share, party favors, etc.) within easy reach of where you're sitting. I need everything in front of me. I can get overwhelmed when I'm hosting, so I don't task myself to remember to retrieve items. If I put the party favors in an out-of-the-way spot, for example, I forget to hand them out. Some might find this kind of prepping over the top, but for my personality type, prepping makes the event less stressful. Do what works for you.

> Allow yourself at least fifteen minutes before salon time to do a walk-through of the house and bathroom (if at an offsite venue like a restaurant or rented room, do a similar walk-through and check in with the staff) and take time to breathe.

## ENDINGS

Endings are an often-neglected and casual part of gatherings. We usually disperse one by one or in small groups when we sense the shift of energy in the room, or in ourselves, and are sent off into the night with a warm hug or wave from the host. There's rarely an obvious cue from the host signaling the event's ending, yet alert guests notice, through the winding down of conversation and the host's body language, that the time has come to call it a night. For the most part, casual endings can be fine, but when something doesn't go well, it can affect how you feel about everything that went before it. Think about those events you've attended where something went wrong at the end. I was often a witness to bad endings at our bookstore. The bookstore was located right above a beautiful wine and tapas restaurant, one of my favorite places for entertaining authors before their events with us, and the site of my first date with my husband. However, the lot behind our store and this restaurant was privately owned, and despite numerous signs warning about being towed if you parked there without a special permit, restaurant and bookstore customers used it and were towed. The towing company was aggressive and the cost to retrieve your car was well over one hundred dollars. Having to retrieve your car at great expense after a lovely meal or author event certainly tainted the experience, and I was glad when the lot owners changed to a less aggressive company and improved signage.

I witnessed another "not great" ending at the close of a trade conference I was cohosting. The conference took place over four days and featured bus tours, education, an exhibit floor, evening receptions, and keynote presentations. It was a huge success overall, the result of months of planning by two teams working together and numerous volunteers. Unfortunately, though, our final event ended without a formal close. We'd gone over the time allotted, and the MCs quickly wrapped it up. As people dispersed, wandering over to the piles of books and swag gifted to them by our conference sponsors, I couldn't help but wish we'd spent a few minutes acknowledging the talents and achievements of the community we'd brought together for four days, with hopes expressed for what great things might happen next as a result of what we'd learned and discovered from each other. As we plan our next conference, we're building in a formal close, as well as special moments within the program to serve as transitions from one event to another.

Other "bad" endings to more intimate events include your departure being barely acknowledged by the host, or the opposite, when what you hoped would be a quick and kindly "goodbye" turns into the equivalent of a wedding receiving line. To honor the importance of endings for your salon, consider a ritual of sorts to metaphorically close the space, thank your guests for their presence, and signal that they can leave, or linger, after your goals for the gathering have been accomplished.

The need for a formal close is especially apparent when we've discussed a topic that requires a lot of vulnerability. I learned this in a dramatic way when I hosted a salon on the subject of #MeToo, the survivor-led movement against sexual violence. (I mention this experience in the "Troubleshooting the Unexpected" chapter, too, as it was memorable and prompted some format changes.) From the get-go, the atmosphere at this salon vibrated at an unusually high emotional intensity. The first person to arrive burst into tears almost immediately, letting me know how much the topic triggered her. As others filtered in, I sensed a collective tension and unease. We shared deeply that night, and there were times when the conversation wasn't easy for the speaker or those listening. We are a woman-only salon, and each of us had experienced harrowing #MeToo moments involving men.

My husband, who always decamps, either away from our home or to a back room, entered the salon space while we were still closing out the conversation. The salon had run long and he thought we'd finished up. For some, his male presence, after two hours of discussing the various ways the patriarchy had traumatically affected our lives, felt intrusive, and his offer to hug, very unwelcome. It was awkward for him, a lifelong feminist who didn't realize quite what he was walking into, and for the salon members. I understood then and there that I needed to create a closing ritual to help us all transition from discussion to reentry into the non-salon world. He and I also made a plan that he would not enter the salon space until I texted him that we'd officially closed the salon.

I've created a closing ritual that involves three stages. First, I seek the best moment to enter the discussion and state that we've come to the end. Then I pass around a sheet of paper containing quotes by notable people submitted in advance by salon members on the evening's topic. One by one we read them aloud, passing the sheet from one member to another. After the reading, I thank everyone for coming, and we sit for a moment, to feel within ourselves the night's discussion and let it begin to percolate for future contemplation. Guests may choose to stay on after the closing, but as host I've relieved them of any concern about when the right time is to leave. We've lately added a clothing swap after the salon wraps up, which works well as a transition from focused discussion to casual conversation over gently used clothing and accessories.

One last point on beginnings and endings for salons, which I make several times in this book: Begin and end on time. Even if waiting for latecomers, begin on time for those who made a point of showing up when scheduled. Similarly, close your salon on time to respect everyone's schedules. To paraphrase an old saying: Better to leave them wanting more than wondering when they can unobtrusively take their leave. My heart swells when I see the salon members lingering by their cars, talking to each other in the yard or street, before driving away. I love that through this salon, we've created a new community of friends.

# DISCUSSION STYLES

"A good conversation is not a group of people making a series of statements at each other. In fact that's a bad conversation. A good conversation is an act of joint exploration."

—DAVID BROOKS, *How to Know a Person: The Art of Seeing Others Deeply and Being Deeply Seen*

MY HUSBAND AND I WERE enjoying dinner at the home of a couple we adore spending time with when one of them mentioned she'd been part of a short-lived spiritual book club. Although she was really interested in the books they'd chosen to discuss, she'd dropped out of the club after one Zoom meeting. She said that two of the members dominated the conversation, and added, "I'm not really a group person." I wondered if it was more the case that she was "not really *that kind of group* person." I know I'm not! In the chapter "Troubleshooting the Unexpected," I mention the dangers of mic hoggers, who can take down a group faster than you dare imagine. I've witnessed this scenario happen too many times, personally and professionally.

Conversation is certainly an art, whether you're leading or finding your way as a contributor. Who hasn't been part of gatherings where the only way you could participate was to interrupt someone speaking? Although this kind of nonstop conversation is exciting for some, like a fast game of ping-pong, it's challenging for introverts and very polite people. Or consider discussions that are so structured there's no room to explore a topic's side roads for a bit? Oppressive for the creatives. Hosting a discussion-based gathering can at times be like holding the reins of a horse; you let the horse (aka conversation) go in certain directions, giving it the freedom to explore unexpected paths if they look appealing, but you also need to keep an eye on things to avoid any metaphorical electric fences or injurious potholes. You can change your mind about conversational destinations at any time, but you don't want to lose control, unless it's one of those rare instances when that's the perfect thing to do.

How we engage with others in conversation can go so many ways, as can our level of enjoyment. We tend to know what we like, and some of us have more of a sense of adventure, either as leader or being led, which influences our experience. I've found it useful to create a kind of road map for attendees at the beginning of the salon, as most people prefer to know what to expect in gatherings, at least generally. I avoid being too structured about this though, in case I realize it might be good to switch gears mid-event because of something that comes up or occurs to me.

When you think about conversational formats for your salon, prioritize what's important to you. Is it about making sure every voice is heard? A lively conversation with few silences? Intentional quiet moments for reflection? Then consider how you communicate the format to members and keep to it in practice. Remember also that you can create rules of engagement, but if you don't enforce them, they become meaningless.

Experiment with any of the approaches below, or a combination, or your own unique style—it's all up to you! Be prepared to pivot if it's not working, or to step up and lead the group through a rough patch. Sometimes you need to do both. Here are some formats I've observed and used:

**Round-robin discussion.** The host leads with a question, then each member of the group, in an order determined by the host, has three to five minutes (or some other length) for a response. Benefits: Everyone has an opportunity to speak, the structure is very clear, and the moderator is in control. Cons: Some folks might find this to be a heavy-handed structure. The "one at a time" format precludes back-and-forth conversation between salon members, and also might inhibit going deep on the subject unless the host continues with follow-up questions.

Challenges: Folks might go over their allotted time or start speaking with each other, and the host has to interrupt to keep order. This format demands a host unafraid to keep to the rules. **Open discussion.** This is the opposite of a round-robin—members have no rules on length for speaking or taking turns. It's nonlinear, nonhierarchical, and lightly moderated. The host will often begin the open discussion periods with a question or quote on the theme and invite members to chime in. Benefits: Folks can dive deep into the topic, pull in other perspectives, and experience a lively conversation unfettered by direction. Cons: Dominant voices can take over, and quieter voices may be shut down. The conversation could go wildly off topic. As host, you might struggle to steer the conversation in the direction you had in mind while planning. Challenges: The host has to be comfortable letting go, and then knowing when to rein things back in. This format requires the host to scan to make sure every voice is heard, if that is one of your goals.

**Small group breakouts.** This involves breaking up a large group into smaller groups for discussion. Usually each small group is assigned a leader to keep conversation on track and be a timekeeper, but this is optional. Benefits: Introverts are more comfortable in this format, conversations can go deeper and be more personal, and bonding between members is more likely. Cons: You risk losing the larger group perspectives on an issue. Someone can dominate a small group, too. It can be intimidating because it feels more personal and risky. The host has less overall control. Challenges: It may be tricky to break folks up into groups that have a balance of personality types, or to find space at your venue for small groups to go into separate places within a larger room or to a different room.

**Fishbowl.** A small breakout group discusses an issue in the center of the gathering, while the other members sit in an outer circle witnessing. Switch folks in each group at a certain interval to give everyone time in the center. A variation is to stop discussion in the fishbowl circle at a certain interval and invite the observers to offer their thoughts on what they're hearing. Benefits: Everyone is involved in the discussion in some way, so comments are not limited to small breakouts. It is also an exercise in listening and witnessing. This would be a good format for a larger group. Cons: Observing in silence may be hard for some extroverts, and speaking in a small group in front of observers is potentially challenging for introverts. There might be a staged quality to the discussion that risks a loss of authenticity. Challenges: If your group is small to begin with, this might not work, but you could do this with two people talking and the remaining group witnessing, then changing out members to the center.

**Anonymous cards.** The host passes out cards to everyone and asks members to write down some thoughts on the salon theme, or a response to a question on the card. The cards are then put into a basket. The basket is passed around and each person draws a card to read to the group. Another approach would be the facilitator reading each card. After all the cards are drawn and read aloud, lead a discussion about what came up for members. Benefits: This is a great choice when hosting a salon on a potentially triggering topic. The anonymous start to conversation might prompt some more personal daring and sharing. Cons: In a small group, the anonymity of the comments on the cards is questionable, and some folks will not feel comfortable sharing. Challenges: This is a low-risk, high-return way to start off conversation, but it's an unusual approach and can shake things up.

**Presentation by an "expert," followed by a brief Q&A.** This format is old-style salon-ing! Are you doing a salon on sleep? Bring in a sleep expert to talk to your group and answer questions. For other themes, consider a local historian, indigenous representative, musician, poet, chef, theatre critic, politician, etc. If you want to bring in someone from outside of your area, you could bring them in virtually for part of the salon, and then continue the discussion with members after the expert logs off. Benefits: It offers your salon the opportunity to hear from an expert and ask questions, to learn from someone outside their sphere of experience and knowledge. It also provides this expert a chance to connect with others in the community and perhaps develop more professional and personal relationships. Cons: Success hinges on the expert's comfort and skill presenting and answering questions. You may need to pay the expert for their time or offer another incentive. Challenges: As host, you need to be a good moderator between the expert and salon members, to keep conversation flow going, stay on topic, ensure that one member doesn't dominate with questions, and watch the time. Whenever you bring another person to present at your salon, it can be a challenge for you as host as you've ceded control on some level to an outsider. You also have less time for the salon to discuss the subject on their own. Discuss "the plan" with the expert and your members in advance to facilitate it going smoothly, especially if the subject is potentially controversial for your group.

Bridging ideological divides through conversation. Bridging ideological divides at salons can take many formats. You could invite people on opposite sides of an ideological divide—a religious cleric and an atheist, representatives from opposing political parties, folks from different cultures often perceived as "at war," etc., and ask them both to speak to your group (or to each other, in a debate or an "in conversation" format) and answer questions. Or the salon could read a book, watch a movie, or witness art that represents a polarizing principle and then discuss it. Perhaps there is something going on in your community that you sense your group has some "feelings" about. Would you want to have a discussion on this that could lead to action and compassion or at least insight into the views of different sides? Consider the tactic of switching places when folks are stuck in opposing ideological positions. Ask these members to change seats and argue for the other person's point of view instead. Benefits: This is a risky format, but also a way for everyone to see beyond their own echo chambers and experience windows into other worlds. In other words, it's very timely in today's often divisive culture. Paula Marantz Cohen, in her book *Talking Cure: An Essay on the Civilizing Power of Conversation*, emphasizes the benefits of conversations that challenge our views. "To speak to the converted or the entirely familiar is not to truly converse," Cohen writes. "It is to have one's beliefs reinforced; it is self-soothing but not self-developing." Cons: Success depends on the diplomacy and tact of all involved when discussing sensitive topics. Are folks prepared to be challenged? Will everyone behave? Might your salon suddenly not feel like a safe place for members? Challenges: You need to find the right folks and topics to explore together, with respect.

# Troubleshooting the Unexpected

*"Problems are not stop signs, they are guidelines."*
—Robert Schuller

You can plan the heck out of a salon and still things go wrong. I mean, we're dealing with humans who, especially when put into a group scenario, aren't predictable. Nor should they be. Sometimes the quirks that show up make the salon richer, surprising everyone with a window into a different perspective, or a revelation about that person or oneself that is quite profound. I've found that those unscripted moments— around the food table, during the breaks in the program— sometimes spark the most interesting, unguarded conversations that lead to deeper connections.

However, the opposite can also happen. Unexpected or impolite (however unconscious) behavior can throw things off, leading to emails from members who say things like, "We're not here to listen to her go down a rabbit hole for twenty minutes," or "I don't feel safe with that person." It can be tough to witness and deal with. However, you can't ignore off-putting behavior. You're the host; your most important role is to tend to the community you're bringing together and keep things harmonious and respectful. Attendees are looking to you to address anything that goes wrong. If you cringe when something keeps happening, you can bet other members are feeling it, too.

I'm often asked by friends who know about my experience hosting events professionally and personally how I'd handle this or that situation. I share my thoughts, but I'm also upfront that I'm an imperfect host. Things still come up that I've never dealt with before, and my first approach to "solving" it might be awkward. We all keep learning, even practiced hosts. So, don't be too hard on yourself if something happens and you could have done better. Just use whatever wisdom you gained for your next salon. With that in mind, here's some advice on troubleshooting the unexpected at your salons.

## LATE ARRIVALS AND EARLY DEPARTURES

Let's face it, things happen, and even the best-intentioned folks experience life events that cause them to arrive late or cut short their time. A member once texted me that she was going to be late because a bear was blocking her driveway. This is not an unusual occurrence in Asheville. She'd honked her car horn and even used an air horn, which she carries in her car for just this kind of situation, but the bear would not leave for at least ten minutes. She kept me posted, "It's almost hibernation time, so they get a little desperate." I responded, "Best to be cautious." Others just can't arrive on time for anything, or they get antsy before the official close. Although some hosts might not be bothered by late arrivals and early departures, they can threaten the rhythm and flow you work so hard to create. Out of respect for those who do arrive on time and stay till close, some rule enforcement is in order. Number one, and something I feel is important for any event you're hosting: Start and end your gatherings on time. Don't delay the beginning or rush the ending. Stick to your plan as much as you can, for the sake of the salon.

To save yourself and attendees the unspoken "what do we do?" conversation when someone arrives late or leaves early, address this potential issue with ground rules before your first meeting. Your rules might be something along the lines of: If you arrive late, please come in and take your seat as quietly as possible. If you have to leave early, please quietly take your leave.

Making it okay for someone to let themselves in or depart without the host having to greet or send them off at the door protects the host from abandoning their post, and the other salon members from losing focus.

However, if this is a chronic situation with a member, it would serve the salon for you to have a conversation with the "offender." In our salon, I noticed one person's pattern of becoming noticeably agitated toward the end of the salon; she was always the first person out the door. I wondered, "Does she even like the salon?" After watching her do this for the third time, I decided it wasn't productive for me to make up stories around her behavior, so I addressed it with her privately. She told me she had ADHD, which contributed to fidgeting, restlessness, and at a certain point, needing to leave because of impatience or overwhelming anxiety. Once I knew what was going on, I felt compassion for her and appreciated the many ways she *was* making accommodations to be in our salon. If you see folks struggling with timing or any other task that demands attention and focus, check in with them before assuming it's a lack of respect.

### THE MIC HOGGER

Okay, you likely aren't using a mic at your salon, unless it's a big salon, but you know what I mean. Also known as Monopolizer of the Talking Stick. You might quickly realize that you've got someone in your group who, if left to their own devices, would dominate and overshare with abandon. Instead of speaking for a few minutes and deferring to the next person, they take everyone on a long, long journey. When others do get to speak, this person will interrupt or give voice to affirmations (instead of a head nod, jazz hands, or finger snapping), which draws attention away from the speaker. David Brooks, in his book *How to Know a Person*, describes this behavior favorably as being a Loud Listener. I appreciate the liveliness and enthusiasm of loud listeners, but this can be jarring in a salon setting, throwing off conversational flow. In any case, the person usually means well, but they might have become a problem.

Salon topics are meant to provoke discussion, but they are also seeds for further thought and discussion outside of the meetings. There really is no way anyone would be able to say

all they might like to on the topic at hand, nor would that necessarily be desirable for the listeners. In the interest of hearing
everyone's thoughts on topics and establishing a comfortable
conversational flow, you need to strike a balance.

What to do? You could remind the whole group of your
salon's ground rules on sharing space in a conversation and not
interrupting others who are speaking. That's what I did as a first
pass at the problem. Or you could suggest folks change up their
communication styles at the salon. If they're the kind of person
who immediately jumps in to answer a question posed to the
group, ask them to hold back, accept periods of silence within
the discussion, and let others be first. This gives space for the quieter folks to contribute. Failing that, as a last resort, you could
use your green ceramic gnome, Gnomie, as a talking stick, which
enables you to walk across the room, wrest Gnomie from the
mic hogger, and pass it on to the next person, as I did in an
admittedly weird passive-aggressive-use-of-a-gnome-to-avoid-
conflict move. Or you could speak privately with the mic hogger,
which is what I eventually did, and really made the most sense.
However you decide to deal with this, the situation must be
addressed ASAP for the sake of the group. This particular issue
is the number one complaint I've heard from members and from
friends who attend other groups (and may have stopped attending for this very reason). Hopefully, a kindly come-to-Jesus talk
with the offender about salon rules of engagement should clear
this up. If it doesn't, the person may have to leave the salon or
you'll risk losing other members, too. We'll address ways to
approach asking someone to leave later in this chapter.

## TRIGGERS

Sometimes things get emotional, and a salon is not a therapy
group. At least mine isn't (see more below). It's important that
your salon be a safe space for all, as safe as you can manage
within your abilities. In interviews for this book, Black Swan
Salon members reported that our "rules of engagement," out-
lined in the chapter "Elements of a Successful Salon," have
been vital to respectful conversation and feelings of emotional

safety. However, it's impossible to guess what everyone's triggers are since they are unique to our life experiences, and if a salon topic is particularly sensitive, like #MeToo, expect that some folks might be triggered. As host, you're wise to watch the energy in the room. Talking about difficult things is challenging and vulnerable. Offering support, which can be simply listening, is usually helpful. Suggesting that everyone sit with the emotions coming up, including the tears, for a few moments might strike you as the best way forward.

I've found that people, including myself, hold back tears too often, and a good cry among friends can be very cleansing and ultimately strengthening. If you've picked your group well, you'll support the suffering person in ways that will help them in their healing. Perhaps they'll realize they have more work to do in therapy, or that they need to leave their spouse or job (or both), or it's time to let go of some long-held regret or bitterness. Over the years I've hosted salons, folks have shared things that brought tears from the speaker and those attending. It's an honor to be in the presence of that vulnerability, and perhaps because many of us have done a lot of personal work, we recognize the sharer's courage. Acknowledging their courage would be a very supportive response. Our salon needs no prompting to do this, but if yours does, as host, you can always step up first.

I've learned from experience that a salon that deals with a tough subject needs a formal closing ritual. For us, this involves reading aloud quotes on the salon's theme, submitted in advance by members. We might even hold hands in a circle, or if meeting virtually, are quiet for a moment as we absorb what we've shared during the salon. Then I end the salon, inviting anyone who wants to linger to do so.

If at the end of a salon, someone is emotional in a way that concerns you, as a good and sensitive host you might inquire if they need a ride home, or if online, if they have anyone to talk to after they leave the meeting. Be generous with your time and heart at such moments. In salons, you're often going deep. Embrace all that implies, and handle with care.

## THIS IS NOT A THERAPY GROUP

You may discover that some members want to go intensely personal with the salon topic. This is not necessarily a negative, as it's a sign that they are quite comfortable sharing, but if they take more time than allotted and move into areas that seem more suited for a therapy session and could trigger others, for the emotional safety of the group, consider gently but firmly pulling them back to the subject and signaling that it's time for the next person to share. Try a kind but authoritative (in your own words) "Thank you, Sue. I'm sorry to stop you there, but we need to move on to Maya so that we all get a chance to share on the topic. We'll come back to you if there's time."

If someone repeatedly moves into therapy-level commentary during your salons, beyond redirecting the conversation to a different member, consider later talking to the person directly and reminding them that others deserve time to share, and the length and depth of their sharing lies outside of what you intended for the salon.

## IF SOMEONE SAYS SOMETHING OFFENSIVE

It happens. It happened at our salon. It was a comment that bordered on sexist, dropped like a lead balloon, and momentarily shut down conversation. As host, you have choices (and one of them is *not* to blend into the carpet or upholstery to avoid dealing with what just happened). In this instance, I put the comment down to a generational difference of perception (the salon member was considerably older than the rest of us) around what was appropriate. The comment was in the grey zone: Did she mean what it sounded like? I wasn't sure. I didn't want to jump on her comment without reflection and potentially shame her. Instead of quickly shifting conversation away from the awkwardness, I took a pause to create space so I could think about it, and allow for someone to come forward with their thoughts if her words struck them as odd, too. We held silence for a few moments, which happened without my prompting. This was meaningful, as our group is not one for being silent, suggesting to me that others were mulling over her comment, too, or at least waiting for me to address it. After the pause, I asked her to clarify what she meant, and her explanation made me feel much better about her intentions. Someone else then shared quite differently on the same topic and we moved on. I would suggest being proactive whenever someone says something that strikes you as sexist, racist, homophobic, etc. To be an ally to the offended group, address the comment with care, and consider a conversation around it, as a teaching moment. It's always important for the host to do their best to keep the space free from potential wounding, but I've witnessed these challenging moments sometimes lead to deeper discussions and serve your salon in the long run. If you find yourself unsure, as I was, of the speaker's intentions, it never hurts to take a pause, ask for clarification, and then open up the conversation to the group.

## IF SOMEONE IS SIMPLY NOT A GOOD FIT FOR THE SALON

Ugh, this is a tough one! But it could happen, and it's possible the person knows it, too, but isn't sure how to address this with you without hurting your feelings. Possible examples that might have led you to think that this person needs to be removed from the group are:

> They violate the ground rules repeatedly.
> Their interest seems very low; they hardly participate and their attendance has dropped off.
> They resist being led and challenge your hostly plans, even appealing to other members to change the structure you've created for the evening.
> You hear from more than one member that this person is "a problem" and disrupts their positive experience.

Solution: Talk to this person privately, and be an active listener to find out what's going on. Perhaps they have personal or professional challenges that are throwing them off their best social game; that's important for them to realize, and for you to know. They might take a break from the salon, but not from your friendship, until they get a better handle on their behavior. Or maybe they will share that there is something in the format of the salon that isn't clicking with them. It might agitate them to discuss personal stuff with a group of people or they may find structure, including being led by another person, constricting, or something that they are not seeking at this point in their life. Is there something you can adjust for them? Might their behavior be a clue to something you could improve for everyone? Whenever a problem arises in the salon, whether it be someone who is not jelling with the group, or some other issue, it's wise to take some time to reflect on the salon in general. Maybe you've strayed from your salon goals, maybe you're not as motivated as usual. Maybe it's time to check in with salon members to get feedback on how it's going and what might be improved. But you know what? It might not be you at all.

If you do need to ask them to leave, if you've talked to them about the issue and you're not seeing any progress, you can point to your ground rules and your position as host, whose leadership the group is counting on, to gently request they take a break (possibly permanently). Clarity is kindness to all involved in situations like this, so beware of waffling or being vague. Some suggested phrasing: "Your conversational style and the salon's are just not in sync. Though we've talked about this before, I can see that our approach is just not working for you. I'm sorry this didn't work out, but I so appreciate that you gave the salon a try." Or: "I can tell that the ground rules we established are not clicking with you. However, those rules are important to what we're doing. As host, I need to make sure everyone follows them. So, let's take a break from your being a part of the salon, though we could revisit this in the future. Thank you so much for all you've contributed to our discussions, and I'm sorry this is not working out right now."

### WHEN THE DISCUSSION STALLS
Some nights, folks aren't talkative. Or your theme is challenging and members are shy to begin discussion. Here are a few approaches to get the ball rolling:
> Change up your salon format. When I anticipate conversation might be tough, I break up the salon into small groups

and put them in separate rooms (or in corners of the room, if you're limited on space). By making it more intimate, folks, especially introverted folks, are more likely to open up. After fifteen to twenty minutes, bring everyone back and share what was discussed in the small groups. Look at the "Discussion Styles" chapter for more ideas on formats.

➤ Ask folks to bring props. When I hosted a salon about the senses, I asked folks to bring in something that spoke to them sensually. Members brought in soap, a piece of music, artwork, talcum powder, spices, perfume, a soft piece of cloth. We shared about our chosen item and passed them around. This was a favorite salon.

➤ Put yourself out there first. Initiate by sharing your own experience of the topic—not to dominate, but to invite further talk.

➤ Have backup questions in your pocket. Preparation is such an important element of a successful salon and helps you be a more confident host.

➤ Ask different questions. Are you asking yes or no questions, or questions that lead members too quickly or easily in predictable directions? Ask questions that prompt folks to dig deeper and reveal more about where their personal stories and philosophies intersect with the salon themes. Make space in the conversation for members to be truly seen for the one-of-a-kind people they are.

# Making the Experience Richer

"At the heart of celebration is a kind of mathematical paradox: the more we share joy, the more it grows."
—Ingrid Fetell Lee, *Joyful*

SALONS CAN BE AS SIMPLE (folding chairs in a church room, or picnic tables at a local park) or as luxurious (group soak in mineral baths at a local spa, or lounging by a fireplace in thick bathrobes at a lodge) as you want, depending on your goals and budget. And your personality. You're the host, and this is a perfect opportunity to let your personality shine through in the ways you envision and realize the experience.

There are so many social opportunities these days that my advice is to make your salon more time-worthy by enhancing the setting and overall experience. What you're creating has to be more attractive than a bowl of popcorn and the next season of your favorite TV show. Think about what you find appealing in gatherings where folks are engaged emotionally and intellectually, and bring those qualities into your salon. In her book *Joyful: The Surprising Power of Ordinary Things to Create Extraordinary Happiness*, Ingrid Fetell Lee writes, "Our world becomes layered. It contains joys that can be seen and others that lie just below the surface of everyday life. And with each joy we uncover, we are reminded that we are the architects of our own delight." With that in mind, as the architect of your salon, take it up a notch, and make it the kind of event you'd absolutely love attending.

## Salon Foreplay

To get to the heart of an idea and explore it from various angles takes time, thoughtfulness, and even vulnerability and risk. It would be extremely challenging for a group to jump right into a difficult subject without prep, though you could certainly do this if it serves a purpose, like pushing attendees to not overthink something and be more spontaneous. As host, I prefer to guide us into deep discussion through a gentle direction of the conversation. This begins long before we actually meet and is something I think of as salon foreplay. I created a Facebook group (choose whatever platform works best for you) for salon members, and post each salon as an individual event, usually a month or two in advance since we meet quarterly. I enjoy the creative challenge of selecting an evocative image and title to represent the theme. I write up a brief description of the topic and then invite everyone through Facebook and email. Over the following weeks, I will often include a link to an article or book on the topic. Here's an example from my salon "In Praise of Beauty":

> **Description:** Beauty inspires us; it lifts us up, takes our breath away, or causes us to exhale deeply. Merriam-Webster defines *beauty* as "the quality or aggregate of qualities in a person or thing that gives pleasure to the senses or pleasurably exalts the mind or spirit." Beauty is sensual; I've heard music so beautiful it stopped me in my tracks, touched surfaces so soft I shivered, smelled scents that drew me in to another space and time, tasted food that left me speechless, seen things that blew my mind. Beauty is also commonly associated with women and their loveliness. What do you consider beautiful? Do you think of women as more beautiful than men? Do you think about beauty often, or is it not important to you? Let's talk about what beauty means to each of us.

During this time of salon foreplay, conversation begins on our Facebook event page and through group texts and emails.

Members will share articles and books on the topic, contribute thematic quotes by notable people, and reflect on past experiences that touch on the subject. This flurry of communication all lends itself to us not approaching the topic cold at salon time, and encourages a deeper, more personal conversation.

## TEASER & ENRICHER

The "teaser and enricher" is not a sex toy ;), though I suppose it could be, depending on your salon theme. It's usually a tangible object I ask members to bring with them to the salon, something that relates to the topic. For our "Exploring the Senses: What Inspires, Soothes, and Turns Us On," salon, I asked everyone to bring a sensual object that was personally meaningful. We were exploring tapping into the senses, engaging with them more consciously and fully, to slow down and smell the roses . . . or the coffee, or the subtle aroma of a glass of wine. Sensual awareness is a way to ground ourselves, because the senses bring us back into our bodies, and also to spark our imaginations, stimulate creativity, and color our world when we might be feeling grey. My life is richer whenever I'm fully present to the senses, so I was excited to explore this subject with our salon and to see what each person would choose to share.

I've always found scent to be the easiest and quickest gateway to memory. Herbal Essences shampoo and Love's Baby Soft perfume (pink and lemon) remind me of junior high. Red Door and Chanel No. 5 perfumes remind me of my mother. Whiskey breath reminds me of my maternal grandfather. Brisk autumn air scented with dried leaves and woodsmoke reminds me of fall in New England. Pressing my nose into a bundle of raw wool at a craft shop reminds me of the sheep on our farm in the mountains. The list goes on and on! For this salon, I rummaged around in my bathroom cabinet, finding an almost full bottle of Rive Gauche perfume by Yves Saint Laurent. I've saved this bottle for years. I first purchased Rive Gauche on a whim at the duty-free shop in Copenhagen's airport, on the way home from a summer study abroad in the USSR. I don't use the perfume anymore, but whenever I open the cap and sniff, memories of that summer flood back, including arriving at trip's end in sweltering New York City. Wearing a light scarf, and feeling very European and sophisticated, I was greeted at the airport by my boyfriend, who swept me off my feet and took us to get ice cream. I can still remember so vividly being on the streets of the city, the ice cream melting down the cone and over my fingers, as I tried to eat as quickly as I could. It was such a joyful moment, laughing in the sunshine, seeing the smile on my boyfriend's face, feeling great relief at finally being home again. This memory lives on in my bottle of Rive Gauche, decades later.

When we met for the salon, we passed around the objects we'd chosen to bring—a grandmother's talcum powder, a (bracing!) bar of Irish Spring soap, two bottles of perfume from the 1980s (another member brought her Obsession bottle, empty but highly fragrant), a favorite spice in cooking, a piece of soft cloth. We also listened to one member's offering, a recording of the song "Shallow," from the recent movie *A Star Is Born*. It was incredibly moving to group-listen to Lady Gaga's deeply sensual, and at times guttural, singing. While discussing what we'd brought and why they were so meaningful, we laughed, were touched, and grew closer as friends. This salon was a favorite, and I believe a big part of that was making the experience richer by making it so personal.

### QUESTIONNAIRES

Besides the teaser and enricher objects, which happen sporadically, our salons include consistent elements to bring a bit of predictable and comforting structure into the gatherings. One is a questionnaire I create for members to fill out at the salon between our potluck and the general discussion. Composing the list of questions pushes me to do a bit of research on the salon theme and consider how we might approach it. The questions range from personal to a broader societal perspective, and often include one or two that we'll talk about later together. When I distribute the questionnaires, the time spent filling them out creates a bridge between the high energy at the beginning of the salon, when we're all bonding, and the general discussion.

Here is an example of a questionnaire I created for our "Finding and Nourishing Sanctuary Within and Without" salon:

**Brief description:** Sanctuary is defined as a place of refuge and protection. A place where you don't fear for your physical or emotional safety. **Questions:** When you think of "sanctuary," what words come to mind? Where do you feel most triggered, most unsafe? How do you cope with this? What places are your sanctuaries? What is it about these places that offers you a way to find ease, to feel safe and calm? Which senses do you engage or disengage to create a physical sanctuary? Sound or silence, smell or no smell, taste or fasting, light or darkness, touch or isolation? How do you create a sanctuary in your mind? Meditation, yoga, vigorous exercise, mindful breathing, winding-down rituals, ingesting certain substances, using an app? Is your home a sanctuary? Why or why not? Have you ever done a house blessing? **Final thought:** "Each of us has an inner room where we can visit to be cleansed of fear-based thoughts and feelings. This room, the holy of holies, is a sanctuary of light."
—Marianne Williamson

QUOTATIONS

Another consistent element that makes the experience richer is asking members to find and contribute quotes by notable people on the salon's subject. I collate these quotes into a one-sheet we read aloud from at the salon's end. This prompts members to reflect on the theme and find something to share with the group. The activity also engages them in the salon itself, as their choices become part of the discussion. In my interviews with salon members for this book, I discovered that reading the quotes together at the end of our salons is quite meaningful to them for all those reasons, and it helps them get to know each other better based on which quotes are chosen and the ways we react to them. Often the quotes surprise me because they are such a different spin on the subject than I'd considered. If you're pressed for time, consider delegating this or any of the tasks mentioned to other members to invite more collaboration.

### REFRESHMENTS

My salons always begin with a vegetarian potluck that is purely social time. Readers know by now that I love potlucks. We build connections when we share foods, and we are also offering a way for members to contribute to, even be cocreators of, the salon. We may discover that one member loves to cook delicious dishes representing her ethnic background or special diet, while another hates to cook, but is happy to pick up chips and hummus or sautéed kale from a grocery store hot bar. In the spirit of diminishing the number of things I have to track, a lesson learned at our "Emotional Labor" salon, I'm not a big organizer of who is bringing what, which tempts fate and the possibility of five bowls of hummus and no desserts (yes, this has happened). Are you adventurous and willing to say, "Bring a dish," and then see what happens? Experiment with your group; you can always change directions if things go awry (though such times make for great stories later—hummus, anyone?).

However, you and your members might like a night off from dealing with food or obligations of any kind. Would you like to have your salon catered? Ask members to chip in for pizza or order in a few selections from a local restaurant. Consider a desserts-only or bowls-of-different-flavored-popcorn event to make it easy and a rare indulgence at the same time. Or maybe meet after dinner, skipping the food and focusing instead on cocktails, tea and coffee, and some light bites. There are so many possibilities, and for some, food is not even important in a salon setting. A delicious cup of coffee, glass of wine, or mug of herbal tea can be every bit as satisfying when in good company.

How can you make the experience richer by spiffing up the food table? Perhaps you bring out your best china for the buffet spread, including beautifully folded cloth napkins and silverware, all set on a lovely tablecloth with candles and flower arrangements, which underscores a bit of formality and specialness to the occasion. Or make it funky with mason jar glasses, a variety of special plates and bowls you've collected over the years, mismatched silverware, and homemade trivets. Or be easy on yourself and use disposable paper plates, silverware, and glasses (not environmentally friendly but helpful when your life is crazy and you want to cut down on cleanup time).

I like to offer guests a combination of formal and funky. When my mother passed away, I inherited her china and Waterford crystal. Though their style is a bit dated, they remind me of the times when she'd set them out for big family gatherings, usually Thanksgiving, Christmas, and Easter. She took great pride in them, and I honor her memory and our family traditions whenever I use them. For my salons, I'll set out a few of her plates and mix it up with special serving dishes that have been gifted to me or that I chose for myself, as well as napkins I made from fabric pieces I purchased at Aldi.

## SETTING

It's really simple and inexpensive to create a rich and inviting setting for your guests. Think about what you can do, within your time constraints and budget, to make your setting memorable. Although we dipped into the importance of setting in the chapter "Beginnings and Endings," we're going to go a bit deeper here. I like to think of all the prep as similar to the work you do before painting walls in your home. You pick out the paint colors, buy the painting supplies, tape off the windows and edges around doors, remove power outlet covers, and cover up the floor and furniture with tarps. This can be tedious and painstaking work, but it makes the painting itself go quickly, and the results beautiful. In the same way, your prep for the salon, especially around setting, will help the actual event go smoothly.

What will your conversation space look like? If you're hosting in a large room, consider moving the seating in closer to evoke a cozier feeling and encourage conversation and intimacy. If your room is small, move some furniture out or toward the walls to create more space and less visual clutter. Do you need to accommodate someone with mobility issues? If so, clear a path for them to a place to sit, and eliminate any tripping hazards (always a good idea anyway). If you have throw rugs or area rugs, use anti-slip tape or pads on the underside to help reduce the possibility of someone slipping or snagging a corner with their foot.

What's your lighting like? My salon happens mostly in my living room, where I have a standing lamp, a table lamp, twinkling string lights, and an overhead light. If the overhead light is on, and I leave to join a small group breakout in our sunroom, when I return I often discover that the remaining group turned it off, those rebels! They don't like it, and I don't blame them. Most people don't like overhead lights unless it's really necessary. Outside of turning it on when we fill out my questionnaires, I try to remember to turn off the overhead light and keep the room softly lit. I cede to the majority and avoid a brightly lit setting.

You can directly shape the salon's energy and mood with music, though take care that it works with the salon's theme and doesn't compete with conversation. I'm very sensitive to sound intrusion, which for me can be sound pollution. I tend to keep the volume very low (or off) once the salon discussion begins. You may have salon members who feel the same way, so do check in with folks. Do you want some instrumental music in the background? Classical? Big band? Current pop hits? The sounds of nature (ocean waves, wind moving through chimes, water running through a creek)? You might consider a flow of music styles throughout your salon to complement where you are in the program, from lively during social time to more soothing and quiet as you begin discussion. Or you might opt for no music; our tastes in music are often so different, and the absence of music allows everyone to focus on the sounds of being social together, on conversation.

One of the easiest ways to enrich a space is to bring more sensual elements to the room. Candles, either real or electric, soften the light and add the suggested warmth of flame. A diffuser can scent the air to match the mood. In either case, make sure your guests are not sensitive to scent, and be careful not to overwhelm with a fragrance. If using a diffuser, I recommend high-quality aromatherapy oils. Citrus scents with a hint of wood (pine, cedar, rosemary, or eucalyptus work well) are uplifting, not perfumy, and smell clean. Lavender and bergamot together are soft and relaxing, and patchouli and frankincense support a meditative space.

Do you want to add some color with throws or pillows? Or be minimalist and clean out the space? How comfy or supportive is your seating? You'll be seated for a long time, so don't underthink comfort for your guests. I've attended events with stiff, unyielding chairs or soft, unsupportive cushions and both were hard on my back and bottom within minutes. Don't do this to your guests if you can help it. Once you've completed prepping for the salon, step out of your space, imagine you're a guest, and then walk in and take in the scene. What are your impressions?

If you're holding the salon at a location other than your home, will the venue's sound system compete with conversation? Sound intrusion was a serious issue with my book club when we met in a bookstore bar. This special place featured two floors of intriguing nooks to gather amongst sumptuous paintings and objets d'art. While we loved this beautiful and inspiring bookish setting, we found it almost impossible to have a conversation, as our voices competed with loud, random music over their sound system. After discovering that the sound couldn't be turned down in our area of the bookstore bar, I went rogue and searched the bookcases for the hidden speaker. When I found it, I unplugged it; I plugged it back in when we were done. I'm pretty sure the staff saw me do this; I like to believe it was okay by them. However, I wouldn't recommend you tinker with a venue's sound system. This was a desperation move for one time only. As it happens, we eventually found a quieter venue where sound was no longer so much an issue.

Will you have some level of privacy if the discussion gets quite personal or loud? Privacy is a must for our group because of what we discuss and the expressed need for confidentiality. Perhaps you can find a venue with a private meeting room, available for free if you support their restaurant or bar with food and drinks purchases, or for a fee that salon members chip in to cover. My community has many spots like this—a tearoom with a private meeting room adjacent, an extra room above a food co-op, a yoga studio that is available off-hours, meeting spaces in community centers and houses of worship. Always consider the aesthetics of the space, as well as accessibility and parking.

Parking is a really important consideration where I live, as available, affordable parking spaces can be hard to come by. Is there ample street or garage parking around your home or at the venue? Is the path from parking to your home or the meeting venue well-lit and easy to negotiate whether on foot or by walker or wheelchair? A salon guest may have a hidden disability, or be dealing with an injury, or have concerns about personal safety if walking back to a car at night. Think about your salon from the point of view of your guests—what might their expectations and needs for the setting be, and how can you best meet them? If you are inviting some folks you don't know well, ask them what accommodations they require, so you're prepared to meet their needs and not make any assumptions.

Another possibility to explore is holding your salon outdoors. During the Covid era, we became accustomed to meeting friends at parks, choosing outdoor seating at restaurants, and going for walks in the woods. As the first winter during the pandemic loomed, my husband and I talked about how we could keep in contact with friends. We DIY-leveled a space in our backyard and created a patio area with a central fire-pit. We staked a few pieces of cattle panel fencing left over from the farm around two sides of the patio, strung sparkling lights, and stacked wood we purchased in bundles from the grocery store. We did all of this for less than one hundred dollars and created one of our favorite spaces to hang out. With a small inheritance from my mother, who passed at the beginning of the pandemic, we added a covered front porch to our home, which we named in her honor: "Peggy's Porch." We bought some cushioned lawn furniture to sit and lounge upon. Both outdoor areas are perfect for gathering in fresh air during spring, summer, and fall.

We've also scouted out other locations. A favorite park has a spacious gazebo with picnic tables and benches. A beloved restaurant offers outside seating in a covered, private alley once used as a passageway for horse carriages. If it works for your crowd and the salon's theme, a picnic in a lush meadow or on a riverbank would be wonderful and memorable. I meet monthly with a group of friends on one of the Blue Ridge Parkway over-looks, about fifteen minutes from my home. We bring camp chairs and blankets and set ourselves up every third Monday to watch the sunset together. I consider this the cheapest "rooftop bar" in town, and the views are just gorgeous. Be imaginative and consider ways to make the experience richer, if only for one meeting, through setting.

## Go the Extra Mile

I credit a teacher in high school with the following idea, which is a favorite of salon members: Write a letter to your future self. I did this with our salon on "Birthing a Dream & Letting Something Go." For this particular letter to self, I was influenced by a wrap-up session at the American Booksellers Association's Winter Institute in Denver in 2016. Led by the Kansas Leadership Center, booksellers participated in an exercise that included writing down a goal and answering some questions about it, similar to those listed below. We spoke our goal aloud to another person and created a dead-line for ourselves to accomplish it. For the salon, I asked members to choose a goal they felt comfortable sharing with another person, then to briefly write down their answers to the following prompts:

> What is something you'd like to accomplish this year? Be as specific as possible.
> Why did you select this goal?
> What are three steps you need to move this forward?
> Who needs to be involved to make this a reality (partner, friends, community partners)?
> What are some challenges you may face, and how might you overcome them?
> List three ways to measure success.

Next, salon members paired off and spent ten minutes each talking about their goals. Lastly, they slipped what they'd written in response to the prompts into a self-addressed envelope that I mailed to them several months later. For the letting go part of our salon, we used slips of paper to write down issues we wanted to let go, and then we burned them in a bowl. My party favor for this salon was, fittingly, a box of matches, to burn down what needs to be let go, and to spark inspiration to achieve goals.

Writing a letter to your future self can be done for any salon, and your members will love it. Before you come to the end of your salon session, ask members to write something to themselves that relates to the discussion you just had. Perhaps it's something they want to keep in mind, or a personal vow to dedicate attention to a certain area of their lives. It could be a description of the journey that lies ahead, a note about how they're feeling at the moment, or a simple affirmation of love and support to themselves. Have them place their letters into self-addressed envelopes that you'll mail to them later. This kind of gift to self, with the excitement of receiving at a mystery time in the future, lends both accountability and intrigue to your salon.

I like to offer a simple parting gift, something with a special symbolic meaning to encourage everyone on their journeys and to thank them for their presence in my life. Party favors add a little thrill and joy to the end of your gatherings, something to take home and cherish. My preference on giving (and receiving) are objects that combine beauty and utility. Party favors have included twined bundles of dried herbs from my garden and bars of soap wrapped up in pretty fabric squares with a card from a Storymatic-brand game featuring comments like "person who says yes to everything," "time traveler," "survivor," and "person who can talk to cows." I've fashioned homemade bookmarks with thematic quotes submitted by members, decorated candles with topical art and words, and offered pocket-size journals containing a slip of paper upon which I've written something to consider (for example, "Forgive someone who has wronged you, and let it go"). For our salon on beauty, when I was short on time, I purchased a dozen red roses and tied cards like "Royalty," "Here Comes Trouble," "Flirt," "Ms. Rainbow," and "Movie Star" to each stem. Whatever rose you chose was your thought or identity for the day, or so I suggested as I handed them out.

Gifts for your salon members don't have to cost much to be meaningful, nor do you need to craft them. You can explore what's readily available at local craft and party stores: mini journals, candles, curios, stress balls, thematic pencils, and more. Although giving is one of my love languages, it might not be yours. If that's the case, delegate party favors to another member who delights in gifting and might also enjoy crafting or checking out the offerings at local craft and party stores. Look for some how-to information on party favors in the chapter "Crafting Party Favors for Guests."

# An Example

"Owning our story can be hard but not nearly as difficult as spending our lives running from it. Only when we are brave enough to explore the darkness will we discover the infinite power of our light."
—Brené Brown

A SALON USUALLY STARTS WITH an idea, and I get my ideas everywhere. I read something, overhear a snippet of a conversation, see a music performance or a TV show, listen to music or a podcast while driving, view a painting or read a book and it prompts the thought, "I'd love to discuss this in a salon!" There are endless possibilities for salon themes. I'll play with ideas for a while, wondering how interested the other salon members would be in the topic, and how we could explore it, before I settle on one.

A recent salon grew out of reading an article in the *New York Times*, "Regret Is Painful. Here's How to Harness It," which struck me as fascinating. Jancee Dunn was writing on the topic of regret, something most of us, if we're honest, have to some degree. She made it personal by citing a regret she's long held on to—she once had an opportunity to stay over at Stevie Nicks's house and opted not to: "Every once in a while, I still think: I should have spent the night at Stevie Nicks's house." Dunn looked to various experts for advice on how we can "reckon with our regrets." One of the experts she reached out to was Daniel H. Pink, author of *The Power of Regret: How Looking Backward Moves Us Forward*. I'm a huge Daniel H. Pink fan, having read several of his earlier books and watched him present at bookseller conferences. I checked out *The Power of Regret* from the library and a few days later, my copy bursting with Post-it notes, I knew I had my next salon topic.

Because the theme doesn't sound particularly enticing ("Hey, Black Swans! Come to my house so we can spend two hours talking about regret!"), I knew this would require a special reveal. When you're taking on a theme that's bound to bring up difficult emotions, I've learned that building up to it and teasing it is best—an example of salon foreplay. In this case, I went ahead and cast out some possible dates for a salon, theme TBA. I wrote the salon members: "I have a theme for the next salon (doing some research now) and hope we can get a meeting on the calendar. Throwing out two dates. LMK what works for you!"

Next up, I kept doing the research. I don't do this for every salon. I've heard from others who want to start salons that having to research and be "the expert" on the theme is too much work, and also intimidating. I get it. You don't have to do that. You can be much more casual and spontaneous when bringing ideas forward for discussion in a salon, or you could make use of the salon starter kits provided here. It's always up to you. But because this theme was close to my heart and would require some sensitivity to build an event around, I wanted tips on how to tackle it conversational style. My end goal always is for folks to leave the salon feeling like they've learned something new about themselves and each other, and to be inspired to keep thinking about the salon theme in ways that improve their lives.

This happened in a salon on friendship. I'd been mulling friendship's many iterations after a conversation with philosopher A. C. Grayling when he visited our bookstore to promote his then-newest book, *The God Argument: The Case Against Religion and For Humanism*. He was working on what would be his next book, *Friendship*. In a conversation over dinner before the event, he described different kinds of friendship, and how these relationships can be more important to us than family and romantic bonds. When I decided to do a salon on friendship, I did more research and discovered that according to Aristotle, there are three kinds of friendships: friendships of utility, friendships of pleasure, and friendships of the good.

Friendships of utility are friendships of mutual usefulness. You can have these with people who provide services for you, for which you pay them (your hairstylist, for example), or with members of a peer support group. Friendships of pleasure can be friends with benefits, or those who share a common hobby or interest, like contra dancing, hiking, or book clubs. Friendships of the good are considered more exalted and are based upon respect and selflessness, loving someone for who they are, not for what they can do for you or the ways they are like you. There are many types of friends—the shades of grey within these three types of friendships: best friends, work friends, lifelong friends, life-stage friends (friends for a season or a reason), codependent and, sadly, toxic friends (are they even your friends?), and so much more.

At the salon, we discussed a tendency many of us share: believing a friend needs to be all things. This expectation can be too much of a burden on a friendship (or a romantic partner, for that matter) and eventually leads to disappointment. One of us mentioned that all her friends are introverts and she's an extrovert. The introverted friends never wanted to go out, which bothered her. Then she thought about the extroverted folks she sometimes hangs out with and how she hadn't considered them "friends." But they actually are; they are friendships of pleasure, and make a positive difference in her life. Not every friendship has to be an exalted friendship of the good. Perhaps we were being too hard on the friends who pass through our lives but play smaller roles. Suddenly, it felt like something life-changing was going on at the salon as we looked anew at the people in our lives, the current ones, the past ones, the ones we might get closer to further on. We resolved to be more appreciative and less judgy about whom we consider a friend. A few folks said they'd try and reconnect with old friends they'd neglected, and others considered reaching out to meet folks who share similar interests through meetups.

Like our discussion of friendship, the rich theme of regret offered potential to prompt looking at life anew, putting judgment aside, even if temporarily, and reflecting on the past within the supportive space of our salon. As we closed in on the salon date, I revealed that it was about regret. I offered a few quotes on regret from famous people, and suggested folks consider their own biggest regrets. I included a link to the original *New York Times* article that sparked the salon idea and referenced Pink's book as source material. I thought about where I wanted to go with this, considering that, after we ate our shared meal, we had about ninety minutes to deal with the topic. I prefer our gatherings to end positively, to allow everyone an opportunity to share, and to plant seeds for further action. Here's how I decided to go with it:

I began by sharing one of my big regrets, one I alluded to in the chapter "Why I Host Salons": I left a prestigious fellowship at Cornell University and threw myself into homesteading on a remote mountain farm. This decision to abandon the fellowship changed the trajectory of my life in so many ways; I was turning my back on my career aspirations, I did not have financial stability (I started this journey living in a tent and eventually graduated to an owner-built farmhouse with no central heating and a composting toilet), and I became very isolated from friends and family. When I made this choice, I was twenty-four, in the final flailing days of my relationship with my college boyfriend, and in the beginnings of a rebound relationship that hadn't gone beyond one night of making out in a car, a mixtape, and several impassioned letters. I certainly wasn't thinking clearly about practical matters.

I'd earned my master's degree in Russian literature and Slavic linguistics, and my fellowship would have provided all I needed—a generous stipend plus tuition—to complete a doctorate. I'd studied Spanish, French, German, and Russian and read broadly about world history and literature in my spare time. I'd long dreamed of becoming an international journalist, living in a rustic but romantically serviceable apartment in some European capital, or a professor in Cambridge, Massachusetts, teaching comparative literature. My dreams could be so specific: I envisioned my Cambridge apartment with wood floors, Persian rugs, thriving indoor plants, a view of Harvard Square. However, I was very lonely and couldn't imagine two more years in Ithaca by myself. I hadn't formed deep relationships with the other students in my department, or with the professors, and I really wanted, needed, to feel secure and loved. My parents were absent in a mentoring capacity, and probably watched my leaving Cornell with sadness and disapproval, but didn't attempt to stop me. This rebound relationship offered, on the surface, a potentially better path, at least emotionally. In the way young people are, I was heedless and romantic, and decided the hell with it and leapt into the unknown, leaving academia, which had long been a familiar and safe harbor, and chose instead to join my new boyfriend. In the Magic 8 Ball I was apparently using then to make big life decisions, all signs pointed to yes.

If I could go back and change things, perhaps I'd have completed my fellowship and sought one of my dream careers as an international journalist, government intelligence specialist, or professor, to combine my love of writing, foreign languages, and visiting new places. I'd also have earned a lot more money. But who knows where that journey would have led me, ultimately? It's all fiction to speculate, and maybe in any of these alternative versions of me I'd have been less happy, or lived a shorter life, or had a breakdown from stress. When I "at least" this decision (using Pink's methodology on resolving regrets we can't undo by reframing them in a way that prompts us to look for the silver lining), I can affirm without a moment's hesitation that I very much value the career I developed as a bookseller, even if it was financially and, at times, emotionally challenging. Bookselling aligned with my bone-deep love of connecting books with readers, and readers with authors. Over the years, I've worked with wonderful booksellers, authors, and publishers, hosted events that were life-changing for me and attendees, became dear friends with many customers, and eventually met and married the love of my life.

When looking over my personal timeline, sorting for the gold, or saddened by the times that were very difficult, I think about the Taoist story of the Chinese farmer, for whom a series of what look like fortunate and disastrous events happen, one after the other. A horse escapes from their farm (bad), but returns with wild horses (good); a son breaks his leg while riding one of the wild horses (bad), but because of his broken leg, is not drafted into the army (good). The farmer does not guess at whether an incident will have a good or bad outcome, despite what seems obvious at the time, because we never know how things will turn out in the end. How life unfolds is a mystery, and unknowable. What we can control, if anything, is how we respond in the moment, to make decisions in the wake of something "bad," to chart a better course, or in the wake of something good, to leverage that into more opportunities for positive outcomes. When I'm in a particularly bad stretch of luck or mood, I try very hard to plant seeds, metaphorical and real, for happier times. Even then, we've probably all felt the truth in the Yiddish expression, "Man plans, and God laughs." But we try. Because of my experiences making rash decisions while young, without real agency or strategy, I've vowed to support any young person who reaches out for mentorship. I know how decisions you make when young, and not just the financial ones, can change the course of your life in ways you may regret later. I want to be a helpful mentor, gently guiding someone towards reflection on the near- and long-term possible outcomes of their decisions, and considerations around life goals, what makes them happy, and whether they may be missing potential red flags or opportunities.

After my regret confessional, I handed out a questionnaire I'd created so folks could begin to consider their regrets and how to address them.

## QUESTIONNAIRE FOR REFRAMING REGRET SALON
Daniel H. Pink, in his book *The Power of Regret: How Looking Backward Moves Us Forward*, identifies four kinds of regrets:
1. Foundation regrets: choices that undermined a basic level of stability, like income and job opportunities.
2. Boldness regrets: regretting the chances we didn't take.
3. Moral regrets: when we behaved poorly.
4. Connection regrets: when relationships fail through neglect or other reasons, and we don't reach out.
> Please choose one or two of the four kinds of regrets and

briefly describe your experience(s).

> When you think about regret, do you tend to go to any of the four kinds of regrets more often? For example, do you have more moral regrets? Or more boldness regrets? What might this mean (if anything)?

> Is there any regret you might be able to "undo" by taking a form of action? For example, if you hurt someone, could you reach out with an apology? If you hurt yourself by going into debt or not saving for the future, could you put in more hours at work to pay down the debt, or create a budget to put a better financial future in place?

> How do you deal with feelings of regret? Take action? Let them go? Ruminate? Block them out? Depends?

> What advice do you give to yourself when you sit with regret? Is your voice compassionate?

> Has anyone tried to make amends to you for a regret they had? How did that go?

## DISCUSSION STYLE CHOICES FOR REFRAMING REGRET SALON

After completing the questionnaires, we divided into groups of four to each share one regret. The small groups offered a chance to share more personally and openly. Each person had five to eight minutes to share a regret, though they also had the option of not sharing, if they preferred. They could use their time to ask for guidance or simply be listened to. Guidance could be along the lines of, can you undo this regret through action? Could you lessen it by looking for the silver lining?

After each small group finished their work together, we returned to the larger group to talk about the topic, with a look at commonalities and differences in our regrets, any observations on what came up, etc. My questions for the group were:

> Does anyone want to share an insight they've gotten from the questionnaire, the small groups, or maybe in their prep for the salon?

> Does anyone want to share if someone else's regret sparked a memory they'd not had in a while, either of something they regret, or of someone doing something regrettable to them?

As a final group activity, I planned for us to write down on a slip of paper a regret we wanted to let go of. We would then add our slips of paper to a small bowl and light the pile of regrets on fire (or flush them down the toilet, whichever is the most effective or even humorous way to move on). However, we ran out of time, so we went straight to reading quotes on regret submitted by members.

This salon was very successful, and part of that, expressed by members, was looking at the idea of regret in a new way. One or two said they originally thought they had no regrets, perhaps because this is how we are often guided to think, at least in Asheville, where an "It's all good!" attitude can feel like a mandate. However, upon reflection, everyone shared different kinds of regrets—regrets around how we treated someone in the past, or about former marriages, career decisions, even how we've treated our bodies. It was interesting to flip the script and consider those times when someone tried to atone for something regretful they'd done to us, and how we responded. Were we kind in our response? Was the interaction helpful for letting go of any ill will?

One of the questions I put to myself was whether I'm compassionate with myself when I sit with regret. I used to be angry at my youthful choices, but now I forgive the younger me. I was doing the best I could. Aren't we all, most of the time?

Because I held this salon in fall, I pondered what kind of seasonal party favor to hand out. My husband and I have customized the glass containers of pillar candles (sold as blanks at crafts stores) with words and images we cut out from magazines and newspapers and then glued onto the glass. To bring light to a darkening season and heavy subject, candles seemed perfect, so that's what I did. My sisters were visiting for a family gathering and we spent our last night together crafting the regret candles. We talked about some big regrets, and how we could address them—by undoing, by apologizing, by finding the silver linings. The healing energy of our conversation went into the candles, and my hope is that it also made its way into the hearts of the salon members as they took them home.

# CRAFTING PARTY FAVORS FOR GUESTS

"Art is the imagination at play in the field of time. Let yourself play."
—JULIA CAMERON, *The Artist's Way*

ONE OF MY FAVORITE ACTIVITIES when preparing to host a salon is making party favors. I think of it as both meditation and creative play, a path to insights and strategy as I mull over my plan for the salon. It's also a refreshing way to unplug from the world beyond my home and rest my mind in the lovely space that art brings me to.

My life is overly full of screens. I look at a computer monitor all day for my work, my husband and I watch TV on a big screen at night, and when I go on walks, I might take calls and check email and social media on my iPhone. This screen time is not great for my sense of calm or eye health. I don't need scads of studies to affirm that constant exposure to screens and incoming, often unfiltered, news creates anxiety. I notice when I become irritable at the smallest things and find it hard to wind down at night. It's like my brain is driving down multiple lanes on a busy highway and I'm not seeing any exits. Because this is an ongoing challenge, I've developed what I call my bag of tricks to take care of myself before my mood worsens. Instead of reaching for my phone at the end of the day, I'll pick up a book of crosswords and work on them with a pencil and eraser. Rather than watch a TV show, I'll play cards with my husband, or light a candle, put on some soft music, and either journal or flip through some printed magazines. Some particularly trying days end with a long bath, then putting on jammies and crawling into bed with a cup of tea and a romance novel. Unplugging calms me; when I turn away from the constant distraction of screens, my soul unfurls from a tight bud, and my imagination finds space to blossom. Crafting party favors is a tried-and-true element in my self-care bag of tricks. This nurtures my love of making beautiful, intentional gifts, and offers healing time when I'm not ruminating about past or future worries. My favorite go-tos for party favors are bookmarks and decorated candles. Both of these incorporate the salon's theme in words, which, as a word person, makes my heart sing, and they're useful, as opposed to party favors you might toss or stuff in a closet. I love bringing in friends or family when I make party favors. There's truth in the saying "many hands make light work," and you'll enjoy great conversations while crafting. My sisters were visiting just a week before the salon on regret, and I asked them if they'd help me decorate candles on the theme. As we'd never crafted together as adults, they began with some hesitation but were willing to give it a try. Over tea and cocktails, we sat around the dining room table, looking through old magazines and newspapers, and sharing laughs and rueful stories of regretful experiences, from teenage perms and DIY highlights to one-night stands. We decorated three candles each, and I loved seeing how differently we played with the theme in our art, too. That evening with them is one I'll always treasure, and my salon loved the candles! There was one candle left over, so I have a special memory, too.

## DECORATIVE CANDLES
**Materials:**

> ➤ 8-inch pillar candles in glass jars with no decorations (also called blanks). You can find these at craft and dollar stores.
> ➤ Magazines, newspapers, and old books that you're okay with repurposing
> ➤ Moxy glue and applicator brushes or sponge wands
> ➤ Scissors
> ➤ Decorative tapes, including washi tape, and stickers
> ➤ Craft paper or newspaper to protect your table surface
> ➤ Box or tin to store leftover cuttings

Decorative candles are really fun and easy to make, and the process is as creative as you want it to be. My first experience decorating candles was with my friend and salon member, Constance. We went to a craft night at a place called Fleetwood, a former pawn shop turned curio shop and chapel with an open coffin by the bar. The venue provided all we needed to create different kinds of crafts, including decorative candles. We sat among a group of strangers, including kids, and had so much fun! Constance made a beautiful tribute to Freddie Mercury, and I decorated candles in celebration of life. I was hooked.

**Here's how I do it:**

> Begin by setting down layers of craft paper or newspaper to protect whatever surface you're working on. Then bring out all your other materials to have at hand.

> Flip through magazines, newspapers, and old books and cut out words, phrases, and images that reflect or play off the theme you're exploring in the salon. You may find, as I always do, a ton of potential options from just one magazine. Collect your cuttings in a box or tin to keep them together and away from all the other materials. You can do this step ahead of time if you want to split up tasks. I always have leftover cuttings that I can pull from whenever I'm decorating candles.

> Consider how you'd like to decorate your candle's glass jar. I sometimes circle the top and bottom of the jar with decorative tape, as a kind of frame or container for the pieces, and then apply small stickers here and there.

> Apply the moxy glue on the back of the cutout pieces (words, phrases, graphics) and the washi tape if it's not very adhesive, then adhere to the glass. Your hands can get sticky, so consider having a damp towel handy to wipe off your fingers. There's not a lot of opportunity to move an image around once you've placed it on the glass with glue, so it's best to work slowly and thoughtfully and accept imperfection. Take breaks every now and then while working on a candle to avoid putting too much on it, which can easily happen. Then add to it as you are inspired.

> Allow to set and dry overnight.

### Bookmarks with Quotations

**Materials:**

➤ Two kinds of paper: one to print the quotations on (20-pound weight is fine) and card stock for the bookmark

➤ Ball of thin twine or ribbon

➤ Charms or curios (make sure you can thread your twine or ribbon through them)

➤ Hole punch

➤ Glue stick

➤ Paper cutter or scissors

➤ Craft epoxy liquid gel, clear packing tape, or self-adhesive laminating sheets to laminate your finished bookmarks

These are always a good choice as they are simple to make, and the results can be works of art, "keepers" that you and your salon members will use time and again. I love the weaving together of different elements in this project: matching charms bearing sayings like "enjoy the journey" and "dreamer" with quotes sourced from salon members, then deciding which craft paper or ribbon will enhance the final look. I always ask members to choose quotes that reflect the salon's theme as a way to prep them for discussion and to use for our closing activity, when we read them aloud. For this project, I use those quotes for the bookmarks, too. If time is pressing on you, you can source the quotes yourself or ask one member to rustle up the number you need for your bookmarks.

Have fun choosing the card stock. There are so many designs available, and if you find one that works with your theme, that will really level up the final look. You can find thematic tablets, loose sheets of card stock, curios, and charms by craft designers like Tim Holtz, whose Idea-ology collections could work beautifully with your subject. I enjoy going to craft stores and seeing what's in stock and on sale. We can get stuck in our own lanes of interest and tastes, and it helps and inspires me to see new designs, including the store's staff picks and recommendations.

I make my bookmarks six inches long by two inches wide, so they will fit snugly into most standard book sizes. This leaves a space about four inches long by one inch wide for the quote, which is the star of this show. Format your quotes on the computer to fit into the dimensions of a four-by-one-inch rectangle. Choose a font that is easily legible (sans serif is usually considered best, but experiment with font choices; this is your project, after all). Print your quotations onto your lighter-weight paper. I look for a plain, design-free paper that is pretty, of a color that works nicely with the card stock, and will receive the printer ink well without smudging, so the quotes are legible. Avoid slick or coated paper. You can purchase loose papers at craft stores if you want to take it up a notch and mix and match. Just make sure that when you apply glue to the back of whatever paper you choose, the paper is thick enough that the card stock design will not show through, rendering your quote less legible.

**Here's how I do it:**
- ➤ Print your quotations on lighter-weight paper, then use your paper cutter to cut them into four-by-one-inch pieces.
- ➤ Cut your card stock into six-by-two-inch pieces.
- ➤ Glue your quotes to the card stock, centering within the edges.
- ➤ Place weight on your bookmarks to set and dry overnight. I usually use stacks of books as weights.
- ➤ Laminate the finished bookmarks with either clear packing tape, a self-adhesive laminating sheet, or brush-on clear epoxy gel. This is tricky and I never do it, but if you're brave enough to risk it all, go for it! If not, skip to the next step.
- ➤ Punch a hole in the top center of each piece of card stock (about three-fourths of an inch from the top edge).
- ➤ Trim twine or ribbon to four- to six-inch lengths and thread through the curios or charms. Then thread the twine or ribbon through the holes in the bookmarks and tie off the ends in a small knot.
- ➤ Snap a photo of your bookmarks laid out, as a memory for you. Great work!

## HERB BUNDLES
**Materials:**
- ➤ Six-inch cuttings of herbs from your garden or the store, such as rosemary, basil, thyme, lavender, mint, sage, and more. I

grow roses in my garden, so I add rose petals, too, for color.
> Thin cotton thread or twine
> Scissors

I'm a lifelong gardener, and I love sharing what I grow with my friends. My herb bundles contain whatever herbs I grow that would pleasantly scent a drawer or closet, or be used in a cleansing ceremony, like a house blessing. Because someone might choose to burn my herb bundle, I look for thread or twine that is thin, strong, and free of dyes.

I gather my herbs while they're still green, and choose, when possible, plants that are flowering, like lavender. Even when dried, the flowers add some color and interesting textures to the bundles. If you're not a gardener, you can buy many of these herbs at your grocery store or in season at local tailgate markets.

**Here's how I do it:**
> Lay the six-inch herb cuttings down in a row on a covered surface, with top and bottom edges aligned, like little soldiers. Sprinkle the rose petals over the herbs.
> Separate into bundles of about one- to two-inch thickness.
> Tie each bundle off at the base, and then wrap the string around the bundle working up to the top. Loop around the top and circle again down to the base, and tie off with a secure knot.
> Lay out the bundles in an airy place to dry out, leaving room between each bundle.

Before giving them to the salon members, I like to wrap a band of paper around each bundle with a list of the herbs and flowers used, and their properties, whether medicinal or spiritual. It's a nice touch.

## Soap Bundles
**Materials:**
> Unwrapped bars of hand soap, either scented or unscented
> Premade cards or cardstock cut to the size of business cards
> Tissue paper, wrapping paper, or pieces of fabric

BARRETT                    87

> String or twine
> Scissors
> Paper labels
> Tape or glue

These are a quick and easy party favor. Because folks can be sensitive to ingredients and scents in soaps, I choose ones that are high quality and not perfumy. I pair them with a special note before wrapping. I'm a fan of Storymatic's storytelling card games, and I repurpose their cards to tuck in with the soaps. The cards I select bear words like "poet," "storyteller," "daydreamer," "someone with wings," etc. If you don't have access to their cards, you could print out words or phrases inspired by your salon's theme to use instead.

**Here's how I do it:**
> Wrap up the soap and card with tissue paper, crinkly wrapping paper, or piece of fabric.
> Tie off the two ends with string.
> Tape or glue a label on the front if you want to indicate the scent (or lack thereof) to help folks select what they want. Otherwise, it's a fun mystery gift you can present in a basket. Whichever one a person chooses has a special message just for them.

## CUSTOM MATCHBOXES
**Materials:**
> Plain matchboxes of any size, though 4.75-inch by 2.75-inch preferred
> Two kinds of paper, one to print quotations on, the other to serve as the base, both kinds at least 20-pound weight
> Glue stick
> Paper cutter or scissors

Custom matchboxes are a fun party favor that combines usefulness with whimsy. I still have matchboxes left over from past salons and using them brings a smile to my face. One of my favorites features a quote by J. R. R. Tolkien: "Where there's life there's hope, and need of vittles." You can purchase inexpensive standard 4.75-inch by 2.75-inch boxes of matches, or smaller versions, at your local grocery or hardware store. If you use a smaller matchbox, you may have to forgo using quotes and choose just a word or phrase instead. At my salons, I put all the matchboxes into a basket and let folks choose what appeals to them as they are leaving the party.

**Here's how I do it:**
> Collect quotes on the salon theme in advance from members or compile a list yourself.
> Cut the base paper to dimensions slightly less than the non-striking sides of the matchbox, and glue on both the top and bottom of the matchbox.
> Print quotes on the other paper, then cut out each quote into dimensions slightly less than the base paper glued to the matchboxes.
> Center quotes on the base paper, then glue down on one side of the match box.
> Let dry overnight.

## OTHER PARTY FAVORS

I've created posies, small bouquets with twine-wrapped stems, from flowers in my garden, and spiffed up tiny journals with inspiring "calls to action" tucked inside. As is obvious by now, I tend to create party favors that blend beauty with utility, a bit of mystery, and, when possible, an inspiring prompt or affirmation. There are so many things we can buy, but it's truly special to receive something that someone put loving intention into. Let us all put special magic into the parts of ourselves that we offer others. Like fairy dust.

If crafting is not your thing: Outsource. For many, crafting is not pleasurable and can feel like one more thing to do. However, if you really like the idea of these party favors, ask one of your salon members to be the party favor creator. They may love to be this person and contribute in this way. When I was interviewing my salon members, the party favors came up often as favorite parts of the salon, with one member calling them "deep gifts."

# TIPS FOR HOSTS

WHEN I SHARE WITH FRIENDS that I host salons, many of them bring up bad experiences they've had in groups and ask how I'd handle them. I always start with my admission that I am not a perfect host. I'm still learning and will be my whole life. Stuff happens that I don't expect, and I find my way through it as gracefully as I can, but I also have my "lessons learned" moments, when it's clear I could have dealt with something so much better. I'm always walking the path of balancing receptivity with authority, respect with guardianship, shyness with leadership.

Sometimes a member is going to push a button for you, or for someone else, and, wow, you've got potential drama to deal with. Or you're dealing with a talker—they might be very entertaining, but they're dominating the conversation and you need to rein them in stat. Or someone is not having a good time and clearly telegraphing that with their body language to everyone in view. And then there are the times when a member suggests a change of plans in the salon format to the whole group, which conflicts with your plan and agenda. It can be tough and challenging, but my goal with these suggestions is to help you host with confidence.

Here are some hosting tips that have proven useful:

> Select your group well. Each person in a salon is a special

ingredient in what you are creating together. If you know a person to be a disrupter, do you want them in your group? Maybe you do, to shake things up and invite new perspectives on salon themes. But maybe you don't? Maybe you're seeking harmony (but never blandness!) among folks, and mutual respect. What's the vibe you're looking for? Choose wisely.

> Think about what you're projecting through your presence and your words, and how you communicate to salon members. I'm often reminded of the importance of crafting narratives about ourselves and our experiences that are not self-deprecating and diminishing. Not false narratives, but also not the often-dismissive ones we, especially women, can come up with to downplay achievements and diminish our bravery, risk-taking, and sacrifice.

> Ask guests to leave their phones in their coats or pocketbooks or a basket you provide. Sherry Turkle, in her fascinating book *Reclaiming Conversation*, writes about the science behind how the presence of a phone will affect in-person gatherings: "Rich conversations have difficulty competing with even a silent phone. To clear a path for conversation, set aside laptops and tablets. Put away your phone." If someone needs their phone nearby because of a family or emergency work situation, ask them to silence it and put it out of view (but where they could feel the vibration) so it doesn't affect the others. This approach is also a way to keep the salon confidential if that's important to you and your members: no phones, no recordings, no photos. We do not take photos at our salons unless everyone agrees it is okay.

> Consider creating a private members-only Facebook, Discord, or other online group where you can share important event information, post group "rules of engagement," upload photos from your gatherings, and keep conversation going between meetings. This is also a great way to archive a history of your gatherings. If you do this, you'll need to monitor it, and lay down some online rules as well, if necessary. I have a private Facebook group for my salon,

but some members are not on Facebook. I make sure to email the entire salon the details for each meeting, so no one misses out. However, those not in the Facebook group *are* missing out on the history and immediacy of response in a supportive online community.

> Take a pause before intervening or responding to a potential issue that comes up either in-person or online. This is a good thing to do in all spheres of life, and I'm always working on it. I'm reminded of Viktor Frankl's quote, "Between stimulus and response there is a space. In that space is our power to choose our response. In our response lies our growth and our freedom." Sometimes a suggestion to switch format mid-salon is actually perfect and you need to get over yourself and your plan and go with it. Sometimes a pause allows someone else to speak up and say something they need to say. Sometimes a few breaths allow you the clarity to deliver the words you need to. I've never regretted the pause.

> Deal with a problematic person in the moment with kindness and respect (cut them off gently but firmly if they are dominating, for example) and then speak with them privately about the issue if it's a recurring one. I can be conflict avoidant, so I get why for some this is really hard to do, but for the sake of the other members, do something.

> Incorporate introductions into the more social part of your salon, or at the beginning. I personally am uncomfortable and want to run out of the room whenever someone says, "Let's go around the circle and introduce ourselves," but as a host, I endorse introductions because it can be grounding for the group. Introductions are only necessary when you first start your salon and when you bring in new members. When you decide to go for it, be clear on how brief folks need to be when sharing their bios. Some people could easily spend ten minutes introducing themselves, but if you multiply that amount of time by the number of members, you might spend an hour on introductions. That's probably not your best use of time. I advise folks to stick to a two-minute elevator speech, max.

> Don't be too heavy-handed when directing folks; you might miss something! Within the time frames I allot for each part of my salons, I allow some wiggle room for spontaneous conversational exploration, leaving space for introspection, for the "You know what that just reminded me of?" Some of these off-the-cuff moments are the most delightful and revelatory.

> Always provide nonalcoholic beverages. For so many reasons, folks may not want to drink alcohol, and they needn't explain why. I always offer coffee, tea, and water infused with fresh fruit, as well as wine. Some of my salon members love white or red wine, but others don't drink at all. I'm a teetotaler and am grateful when the host provides a refreshing alternative to alcohol, and something that's more than just water (which is lovely, but seldom feels like a treat). My next-door neighbors, who own a brewery, make a carbonated herbal tea with holy basil (tulsi) and peppermint, a delight! Maybe you can find something similar that offers the celebratory or kickback feeling of alcohol, without the alcohol. Your guests will appreciate it.

> Laugh at yourself, be kind to yourself, and be proud of yourself, however it goes. Soak in the joy of a wonderful experience that YOU made possible. Our salon members do many things socially, but none of them gather for this kind of focused, participatory discussion. As I researched this book and interviewed salon members, it was clear how very much they love our salons. The salons, and the community that we've built together within the spaces of our gatherings, have improved all of our lives. You're doing something big, brave, and risky (it is always risky to host) and putting yourself out there. Good for you!

# Tips for Attendees

Have you been invited to a salon? The salon might be very different from what's described here, but likely there are similarities, or at the very least, a focus for the event. If you're interested in the topic and looking for a new thing to do, stretch yourself and give it a try! Here are some general tips on being a guest at a salon, to improve the experience for you and the host.

> Inform the host in advance if you require any accommodations, such as mobility requirements, supportive seating, or hearing, scent, or lighting considerations. The host can investigate whether the venue, or their home, will work for you and make adjustments.

> Arrive on time. A salon is usually a focused discussion and not a casual get-together; likely the host has a plan, which includes timing. If you're going to be late, ask the host if they'd like a text to let them know your ETA or if they'd prefer a quiet late arrival.

> Respect the host's plan for the evening. To use a metaphor a salon member shared once, let the host drive the bus. Don't try to drive the bus. Unless otherwise stated (as in, the host is floundering and asks for help, or has stated that this is going to be an organic, group-led event and requests feedback and input) this is not a consensus experience; it's likely

host-led and they have a plan. Your in-the-moment ideas on how to do something differently might not be welcome.

➢ Don't be "that person." Read the chapter "Troubleshooting the Unexpected" to learn more about mic hoggers and other problematic behaviors to avoid.

➢ If the salon topic is one on which you're an expert, alert the host in advance (they may love any guidance you have to offer in prepping), but if not asked to present on the topic at the salon, please refrain from dominating.

➢ And, in this vein, salons are not places to network your professional services, unless that is the theme or explicit purpose of the salon.

➢ Ask the host if there's anything they'd like your help with. Maybe they'd appreciate assistance prepping for the salon, crafting party favors, scouting venue locations, or, if at the host's home, clearing dishes and cleaning up at the end.

➢ Arrive with an open mind and heart. Many of my salon members were unsure what to expect at our first salon, but they gave it a shot and most of them come back every time. A salon may be unlike anything you've ever done before. Be open, and then be proud of yourself for taking a risk and showing up.

# Variations on Salons

# From Book Club to Salon!

"Books are something social—a writer speaking to a reader—so I think making the reading of a book the center of a social event, the meeting of a book club, is a brilliant idea."
—Yann Martel

I'VE HOSTED BOOK CLUBS FOR almost two decades, beginning with one named "All Romance All the Time" (ARAT), where we explored romance through different genres—sci-fi, mystery, young adult, fantasy, historical fiction, and more. At the time, I co-owned and managed an independent bookstore. My favorite part of the job was chatting with our customers. Every day was a surprise party, as I never knew who would walk in the door and engage with me on books or whatever else was on their minds. I learned so much about life from these brief encounters. One poignant exchange happened shortly after my father died, which I'd shared about in our store's email newsletter to customers. An older man came into the store and reached across the counter, taking my hand. He said, "After a parent dies, it's not just one big change. Everything in your life changes a little bit, too. It's a huge adjustment to grieve." I hardly knew this person, yet he knew my heart at this moment.

During my bookseller years, reading romances was perceived as a guilty pleasure many customers chose to keep closeted. If you were going to read genre books, the thinking then was (and still is for many) that mysteries were a more respectable choice. In my righteous moments, I viewed this as a reflection of our society's preference for violence over happily-ever-afters, but as an independent bookseller, I supported folks in whatever choices they made for their reading pleasure. Our store didn't have a romance section (yet!), and I noticed that often when a customer would order a romance, it was on behalf of someone else—an elderly aunt, their mother, the neighbor to whom they owed a favor, a sick friend. I could tell when I asked about their "friend's" favorite authors and kinds of romances (Enemies to lovers? Nerd in shining armor? Historical? Paranormal? Spicy? Time travel?) that the novels were actually for them. Hoping to take shame out of the transactions, I revealed to these customers my unabashed love of the genre. After they came clean that they loved it too, we'd recommend favorite authors to each other. Eventually several of us decided to formalize our fandom into the ARAT book club. We shared a lot of laughs, swoony sighs, and eye rolls when we met each month to discuss our chosen book. After exhausting ourselves upon the rocks of *Fifty Shades of Grey*, the most unpopular and, as it turned out, final romance for our club, we decided to move on from the genre to a broader focus. We morphed into our current "Women in Lively Discussion," aka WILD, where we discuss fiction and nonfiction by women (cis and trans) and non-binary writers, and read the occasional romance because I'm still a booster of the genre.

Over the years, the WILD book club has expanded to almost one hundred members, though a smaller number meets in person. The core group, the regulars, are incredible women ranging in age from twenties to seventies. Over time and countless glasses of wine and cups of tea, through conversations that grew out of book discussions or happened in the moments before we started them, we've learned about each other's childhoods, families, regrets, triumphs, health challenges, marriage challenges, and taste in books. When the pandemic kept us from meeting in person, we met on Zoom. Having survived that dreadful experience together, and laughing at the irony of discussing *Station Eleven* by Emily St. John Mandel two months into Covid (we'd chosen it the year before), we emerged a tighter group. We currently meet at a rooftop bar downtown, most of us arriving a half hour early to catch each other up on our personal lives.

Being a member of a book club is a commitment. Our time is precious, and devoting a good number of hours to reading the book club selection is no casual thing, especially when it turns out you're not keen on the monthly pick. I've experienced this a few times, thinking, "Who the heck chose this?" only to have to admit to myself that *I* did, and, worse, had inflicted the wretched read *on other people*! Still, it is often the book that doesn't please everyone yields the best conversations, which is something to keep in mind. And expressing your thoughts on the book? That's also a big deal. It can be scary to voice opinions about a book's content and quality of writing in front of others, especially if you don't come from a background where this is a common thing to do, or you're a shy person, or both. Will you be judged? Is it excruciating to admit you hated the book when everyone else is saying they loved it, or vice versa? Do you have fear around speaking in front of a group? So much to consider!

I was a member of another bookstore-affiliated book club that, without expressing it as such, salon-ed through weekend book club retreats. We would meet from Friday afternoon to Sunday afternoon at a conference center a half hour from town. We rented a big house with many bedrooms and bathrooms, a full kitchen, and a central living room with a gas fireplace. The center provided delicious meals, but we also had the ability to cook for ourselves if we wanted, and to bring snacks, which we were all keen on. These retreats took place in the fall, in the mountains, which made our living room setting with the fireplace particularly cozy. We discussed three books over the weekend, plus group-watched a film based on one of the book selections. The weekend was filled with wide-ranging conversations touching on all corners of our lives, and the book discussions went much deeper than when we met for an hour at the bookstore. It was fabulous! I modeled a salon retreat on this book club experience, and it worked like a dream.

Book clubs, by virtue of being a forum for discussion, are the perfect group to springboard to a salon. If all goes well, it can be like kicking off the training wheels and sailing ahead on your bike, enjoying the ride. Book clubs have everything going for them: Folks are used to showing up at a venue to meet, they bring their world views and opinions, they've been part of group conversations on one subject (the book), they likely have experience being led by a moderator, and, odds are, they're seekers and lifelong learners. If your salons require a bit of prep and research by the members, they're used to that because they read (most of the time) the monthly book club selections. When I decided to start my salon, I asked a couple of book club members to be part of it. When I need more salon members, I look there again. I've seen them in action, and they fit right in.

If you lead or are a member of a book club, dip a toe in the water by suggesting a salon on a subject that arises from one of the books you're reading together, or may choose to read together, if you're inspired by it as a source for discussion. Many of my salon themes are the direct result of inspiration from books I'm reading. Invite book club members to dig deeper into the topic. As host, consider the many ways you might make the experience richer than what's currently happening at your meetings.

### AUTHOR-CENTERED SALONS

The simplest book-club-to-salon transition is hosting an author-centered salon. Start by involving authors living in or visiting your community. Check out your local independent bookstore's author event calendar to see if an upcoming event features an author, or book, that looks like a great choice for a salon discussion. My number one tip: Purchase the author's book at the host bookstore. *Do not* purchase the book elsewhere. If the store is out of it, order from them. By financially supporting your local bookstore this way, you're directly supporting their mission to bring authors to your community. If you build a positive relationship with the store by supporting their author events with purchases, you may be tapped for special meet and greets with authors before events, as well as other outreach and benefits that stores extend to their favorite customers. Don't be shy about asking the bookstore if they will offer a small discount to your club to incentivize members purchasing from them, though be aware they may not be able to do this. And ask if they sell audio versions, since many of today's book lovers prefer to listen to rather than read from physical books. Here are additional tips and ideas for an author-centered salon:

> Ask members to read the author's work, attend the bookstore event, and then meet afterwards at a nearby restaurant to discuss the work, the author, and the topic more in depth. If you can match a restaurant's cuisine or ambience with the book's theme or setting, all the better.

> Find out from the bookstore if you can invite the author to meet with your group before or after their event. This is often possible and offers your salon members special access to the author in a more intimate setting. It's like a backstage pass, or VIP preshow event, an experience to remember and share on social media. If taking the author out to a restaurant, you're expected to cover their expenses and provide transportation unless the author states otherwise. You also need to make sure the author gets to the store event in time.

> If the author lives in your community and is not on a book tour for their new book, ask your local bookstore for their contact info, or contact the author directly to see if they would be interested in presenting to your salon in-person. Tapping into your local author community is a great way to find experts in fields and literary genres your salon may be interested in exploring.

> If you can't meet with the author in person, inquire about the possibility of a virtual visit. When our book club does this, we host the author first, and then after the author logs off, go deeper into the book or any themes that come up.

## MORE BOOK-CLUB-TO-SALON IDEAS

> Enjoy a meal together inspired by the book. Create a referenced meal in the story or one that celebrates the setting. My husband is a big fan of author Donna Leon's Brunetti mysteries, set in Venice, Italy. He loves to make, and I love

to eat, *risi e bisi*, Venetian rice and peas, a meal beloved by the title character, Commissario Guido Brunetti. This dish is so good I could celebrate it all day. What fun to connect literature with cuisine! You could go out to a restaurant, prepare the meal yourself, or do this as a potluck, with everyone bringing a thematic dish.

➤ Discuss elements from the book (culture and mores, themes, relationships between characters, the genre) in connection with your local community or lived experiences. Is the book a mirror of your community? A window into a different world? Are there issues happening in the book that are happening in your community? Do you relate to certain characters? Do they remind you of people you know? Does the book bring back memories?

➤ Group-watch a film based on the book and compare the two for how they express the story. What does the film emphasize, skip, or add? Which was a richer experience for you? The prevailing belief is that books are always better than their movie counterparts, but many, like me, view the film as a separate work of art, to be viewed on its own merits. Can you do that?

➤ Read a scene from the book together, with members speaking the lines of specific characters. Perhaps you might dress "in character" for the reading. Is this a period piece? If contemporary, does one character always wear corduroys and cardigans, or are they quite chic and love a red lip? Have fun acting out the scene and becoming immersed in the author's created world. Then discuss the scene more in depth. What came up for folks? Did hearing it change how readers understood the scene or certain characters' points of view?

➤ Attend or find online a performance of music referenced in the story, or that is perhaps even central to it. Does this affect your reading? Your appreciation of the author? Your own tastes? Some authors provide a playlist of music that inspired them while they worked on the book. Share that list with your salon members and discuss where you see the music popping up in the work—where you spot the influences.

> Is there an art exhibit, artist, or specific work of art referenced in the work? This can be the starting point for a discussion on art and literature, beginning with the book. For example, Tracy Chevalier's novel *Girl with a Pearl Earring* is based on a famous painting by Johannes Vermeer. Perhaps you could center a salon around this book and invite an art historian to discuss Vermeer and the Dutch Golden Age. Then group-watch the movie adapted from the book.

> Is there a nonfiction book that addresses a topic you're interested in? For instance, the wonderful *Absinthe: History in a Bottle* by Barnaby Conrad III could form the basis for an evening that involves drinking absinthe and discussing the many artists, poets, and writers who created their masterworks while under the influence of this controversial drink.

> Are you the host or a member of a cookbook club? At cookbook clubs, members choose a cookbook and then prepare recipes from it to share and discuss at a gathering. Add more depth and focus to your cookbook club (if you don't already do this) by going around the world through cuisine, spending time after the shared meal discussing the cultural roots behind the recipes. Invite local chefs or restaurateurs to speak to your club about the dishes they love and the reasons why. Explore your group's passion and curiosity around food: Is their love of food, cooking, and sharing meals a lifelong passion? Something new? Typical of their culture?

> Want to go a step further? Set up a weekend retreat at a local conference center, lodge, or B&B, with scheduled opportunities to discuss a book (or books) and get to know each other better. This might be the launch of your salon!

If you're creative and look around you, you will find many inspirations to take your book club discussion to deeper levels and have a fun, enriching salon. Like so many great things in life, it all begins with a book.

# ONLINE SALONS

"If time, so fleeting, must like humans die, let it be filled with good food
and good talk, and then embalmed in the perfumes of conviviality."
—M. F. K. Fisher

D URING THE COVID ERA, I shifted our in-person salons online.
We already had a private Facebook group and emailed and
texted each other regularly about issues coming up in our lives.
We weren't shy about communicating virtually. Besides, we
needed each other. If ever there was a time to connect and share,
a pandemic involving social isolation, a national lockdown, and
civil unrest made any kind of gathering timely and supportive.

Most members hadn't spent much time video-chatting pre-
Covid, but my professional work regularly involved virtual
meetings. I was very comfortable hosting our salon virtually
and helping the others get used to any technical challenges that
arose, like logging on and adjusting their video and audio settings. We now meet at my home again, but if for any reason in
the future, from another pandemic to bad weather, we need to
cancel the in-person gathering, we can still connect and experience meaningful community online.

There are many other reasons one might hold salons online.
Perhaps you want to gather folks—friends from school or family members—who relocated to different areas. Or you want
to do a salon with professional colleagues who live across
the country or in a different country. Or you'd like to host an
expert at your salon and it's more comfortable for the expert
to speak to your members online, in the same virtual room,

rather than to speak to an in-person crowd staring at them on the computer, a scenario that reminds me of the view screen on the bridge of the *Star Trek Enterprise.*

The Three Sundays Series by Anglo-Irish poet and naturalist David Whyte comes to mind as a perfect online salon-like experience. He presents on a theme over three Sundays, offering a mix of poetry, storytelling, and philosophy before taking questions from listeners around the world. He's a brilliant, inspiring speaker, and because we're listening live, there's more dynamic energy in the gathering than there would be listening to a recording, though those are available as well.

Online salons, by their very nature, lack the intimacy and tangible sensual elements of an in-person salon. We're not sharing food together, smelling the delicious dishes brought, touching through hugs, enjoying the scent of someone's perfume, or listening to each other's voices directly. You can counter that with a bit of planning and collaboration from members. Some ideas:

> Schedule a meal into your virtual salon. Ask members to enjoy some social eating and chatting time before you begin the official salon discussion. Suggest a thematic meal (let's all cook a favorite recipe from celebrity chefs Deborah Madison or Yotam Ottolenghi, for example) or be casual and suggest folks just bring what they have on hand to eat.

> Ask everyone to stage their backgrounds. Light a candle and place a vase of flowers within view, use soft electrical lighting, or choose a virtual background that works with the theme you're exploring.

> Suggest diffusing scents—choose a blend of oils or a stick of incense and mail to everyone in advance.

> Play a piece of music at the beginning and close of the salon to set the mood.

> Dress in character or thematically. Everyone wears their favorite (or most goofy) hat.

> Record the conversation for a shared memory and to send to other members who couldn't make it.

## TIPS FOR THE HOST:

> Take time in advance to understand the videoconferencing app you're using. It's kind to your attendees, and supportive of your salon flow, to avoid being distracted by technical glitches.

> Familiarize yourself with your sound, camera, and lighting settings. If you're going to do a screen share, test it out ahead of time. Know how to mute and unmute yourself, turn your camera/video off and on, and instruct attendees to do the same.

> Have a decent internet connection. If you're not at your home when you're hosting, investigate the extent of your bandwidth before the salon starts. You may have to decamp to another space where the connection is stronger or use your phone or a mobile hot spot device as backup.

> Open the app earlier than salon time, in case the app needs to install updates.

> Close any unnecessary tabs to maximize computer bandwidth and avoid any conflicts between apps, particularly if these apps use video and audio.

> If you are screen sharing or demonstrating something, keep the screen share or object still and visible for a few seconds longer than you would in-person, to give people time to focus on what they are supposed to be looking at.

> If the salon is being recorded and/or transcribed, let members know in advance.

> Allow participants the ability to turn on live closed captioning, if that's an option.

> Clarify how you'll run the meetings. Do you want members to use the "raise hand" function, or to actually raise their hands before speaking, or to just go ahead and speak. Video-chatting leaves you with fewer nonverbal cues, and an inability to make direct eye contact, so make this kind of communication easy. You can direct folks to use the chat if speaking is intimidating. Conversely, if you don't need the chat function to support the option of nonspeaking communication, you could turn it off to prevent side conversations.

> Make sure you have privacy for your meeting if that's one of the rules of your salon. Ask members to wear headphones or earbuds if they aren't alone.

> Respect your beginning and ending time. Consider making the online salons shorter than the in-person ones. From my experience, an hour is the longest folks can stay engaged in videoconferences.

### TIPS FOR ATTENDEES:

> Put the video link in your calendar so it's easy to access when the salon is scheduled to begin. Check that you have it well before time, as texting or calling the host for the link at the last minute is distracting for them and can delay the salon's beginning.

> If you're meeting on a platform that you don't usually use, ask the host if you can come on early to familiarize yourself with your sound, camera, and lighting settings. If you're going to do a screen share during the salon, test it out ahead of time.

> Open the app earlier than salon time, in case the app needs to install updates.

> Close any unnecessary tabs to maximize computer bandwidth.

> Mute yourself when not speaking.

> Make sure you have privacy for your meeting if that's one of the rules of your salon. Wear headphones or earbuds if you can't guarantee being alone during salon time.

> Do what you need to do to be comfortable. Maybe you need to turn your video off and use an avatar, or ask others to stop moving so much (I was once in a virtual meeting where someone was walking on a treadmill; it was SO distracting and created a sense of vertigo). Explain your needs in advance to the host so they can make sure the platform, and the behavior of attendees, will accommodate you.

> Show up on time for the salon. Don't leave others waiting.

# THE BLACK SWAN SALON

# MIRACLES FROM THE BLACK SWAN SALON

> "You must till the soil of your friendships both in the good and bad
> times because there will be moments in life when there is no place
> you can walk, cry, and feel safe except for the garden you and your
> girlfriends created."
> —Shenequa Golding, *A Black Girl in the Middle: Essays on
> (Allegedly) Figuring It All Out*

WHO CAN PREDICT HOW YOUR salon will evolve? Like a
garden you design, plant, and tend to, it will develop
organically, sometimes in surprising ways, because that's what
community does. You give your salon the best start you can,
your positive energy and attention, and it will continue on outside the influence of your guiding hand and presence. In my
salon, the chemistry between members, the unexpected conversations, the friendships that blossomed and flourished beyond
our gatherings contribute to an understanding among us that
we have something very special.

I didn't realize how deeply the salon had affected members'
lives until I held a very special birthday party. The format was
inspired by a friend who'd turned seventy-five two years earlier. When she invited me and my husband, Jon, to her birthday party, she let us know it would be a kind of living wake.
In a living wake, friends and family gather to celebrate a person's life while that person can still hear and appreciate the
kind words we would otherwise reserve for a funeral service
or at the beloved's graveside. Often held for people experiencing terminal illnesses, living wakes are also organized to mark
and celebrate milestones in people's lives, including significant
birthdays. After attending my friend's living wake birthday
party, I saw the possibility of living wakes being a version of

115

Frank Capra's marvelous movie *It's a Wonderful Life*. When through an angel's divine intervention, an entire community shows a suicidal George Bailey that his presence and actions made such a positive difference in their lives, he understands that he is loved, and that his life has had purpose. A living wake can serve this same need.

When Jon asked me what I wanted to do for my "arrival of a new decade" birthday, I told him the best gift he could give me was a living wake birthday party. Ever since my mother died at the beginning of the Covid era, in March 2020, I've been thinking about my life, my finitude, and whether my time here has had meaning. I've experienced waves of existential crisis, which I've navigated through discussions with friends, my husband, my therapist, coworkers, the birds at our bird feeder, the bear trundling down the street, and the darkness when I turn off the lights. Though my logical side knows this stems from my newly orphaned state and my childlessness, the reality of which can mean no lasting legacy, affirmations that I matter are extremely meaningful and sustaining.

Jon asked our party guests to gift me by letting me know how I'd positively touched their lives. At my request, he asked them to write their comments down, as I knew I wouldn't remember details from the moments when they spoke them; I'd be too overwhelmed. At the party, after a round of drinks and some catching up, Jon signaled it was time for everyone to begin sharing. We went around the room, with friends telling anecdotes about how we met and became friends. They recalled special moments when I'd supported them, or inspired them, and times when we'd shared a big laugh over a ridiculous mishap or misunderstanding. It was all I could do to keep my heart from bursting with joy and gratitude, and I held back tears many times. It was one of the most moving nights of my life, and now I have their written words for those days when my doubts will inevitably rise up again. What a gift!

During this sharing, the salon came up time and again. I realized that it had changed all our lives in very tangible ways and was the keystone that connected most of us present. As

I looked at my salon mates' dear faces and listened to them speak, a sense of how deeply we'd journeyed together as friends, as seekers, and as sisters washed over me. I was already researching for this book, but the party reinforced a notion that I needed to dig deeper into their stories, as there was much more going on than I knew about. And so began my interviews with each member, where I learned about their salon miracles.

## The Blue Sweater

I interviewed Kathryn, who now goes by Ryn in honor of her last season of life, at her log cabin in the woods. She's a composer and artist, and my former flute teacher. Other salon members regard Ryn's comments at our gatherings as next-level insightful and from a distinctly unique perspective, so I was especially curious how our conversation would unfold. We sat in the cabin's great room, where she and her husband were married. She had a fire crackling in the fireplace and a beautiful porcelain tea service set out for us. I asked her about her home, which is striking in its architectural and furnishing details, and its setting on the side of a tree-covered mountain. She shared that the cabin was built by three generations of men from one family, using special pine trees harvested in Tennessee. The intention for the cabin was to be a place for one of the men to live out his entire life.

She said, "I've lived here now for over fourteen years. My late husband lived here the last twenty-five years of his life. We both had our own music rooms to work, and we'd sometimes make music together in the great room or porch, or his room. This place has a vibe to it: Most people don't even know it exists, and hardly anyone ever comes here. My late husband had a high-profile career, traveled and performed for a living; he needed privacy when he wasn't onstage. As an introverted composer, I relish the quiet and seclusion it provides in a beautiful natural setting. I love listening to the sound of the wind change throughout the year based on how the wind does or doesn't move through the leaves as it flows down the valley and up the curves, swirling around the mountains."

Her salon miracle relates to the clothing swap that we end our salons with, and how a found object became a source of great comfort and support. She shared her story about the unexpected significance of a blue sweater.

"You know, if the only thing that happened in the salon was the clothing swap, I probably wouldn't have ever attended. Initially, I felt challenged by the idea of a clothing swap because as the youngest of both my immediate and extended family, a significant percentage of the clothing I wore growing up was outdated, hand-me-down clothing which I felt very uncomfortable wearing. The idea of once again being in secondhand clothes was very triggering and difficult for me. However, the side effects of our salon clothing swap, and things that have happened afterwards, have been meaningful. They actually helped me get over some hang-ups I had about wearing used clothing.

"The first time we had the clothing swap at the salon, I thought, 'Okay, well, I'll just bring this blue sweater home and see how this works.' Shortly after that, my father died. I kept wearing that blue sweater. It was really comforting to know that it was from one of my sisters in the salon. And more than that, I would wear it to help me feel less alone; it was surprisingly supportive. Shortly after my dad died, I went to be with my mom. That was very challenging. I intentionally brought the blue sweater as a source of comfort and I was wearing it a lot. I also brought this shirt I would have never picked out if I were shopping. It was a shirt that I'd gotten from Constance, and I wear it and feel happy with it, because it has her energy. I was just so pleasantly surprised at the aftereffects of wearing these clothes.

"I also appreciate going through my closet to pick something out. If there's something really special that I don't want to just give to Goodwill or to a consignment shop, I like to imagine it on someone in our salon, and so I bring it. Just this Monday, Constance and I got together and saw a movie and Constance was wearing a sweater that I brought to the last salon. It felt great to see her in it and enjoying it. So, in and of itself, the clothing swap is no big deal, but afterwards, it's a nice bonus. Also, it's fun to try things, brought by salon sisters, which I wouldn't normally wear, and also, I am more likely to let go of some things as well!"

## A CANDLE TO LIGHT THE WAY

When I was visiting Laurie, an architect and world traveler, for her interview, I was stepping into the home she and her husband had recently moved to, a downsize to simplify and be closer to community. Her home is a variation on a Craftsman cottage with what she describes as a no-frills interior: flat trims, wooden panel doors, lever hardware. The decor is contemporary and a bit eclectic with antiques among modern pieces. The overall effect is lovely, warm, and elegant. Her beloved cat had just passed, and I could see the cat's toys still out, as if the cat was merely absent.

Laurie had studied in Paris and designed a monument to Anaïs Nin. She romanticized salons and felt connected through them to her inner Anaïs Nin, a bond she explained to me with a humorous twinkle in her eye. She shared that she has been deeply affected by the salons, "discovering long-buried parts of myself that needed the glow of the salons to become apparent."

When I asked if the salon had sparked something significant in her life, she thought for a moment. Then she left the room and brought back one of the "regret" candles my sisters and I decorated for the salon on regret. Hers was a red candle in a glass pillar, covered with words and phrases like "Behind the Hero's Journey," "Secrets to Living the Good Life," and "Advice from Me to You" reflecting the salon's theme, as well as bits of pretty adornments like ornamental tape, stickers, and graphic illustrations.

She held the candle and explained, "This candle is from our last salon. It's burned down so far now that I need a long match to light it. When my cat Claire passed on, I lit it. Claire was a real sweetheart, and lighting this candle was a way to send her love and light on her journey. I always light a candle for people when they pass, so they can find their way. I loved that this candle was red, has a nice faint aroma, and lovely, encouraging things written on it. After lighting it, I put it out on a beautiful stainless-steel tray designed by Philippe Starck, in the living room where Claire spent most of her time."

## LETTING GO AND STARTING OVER

In 2019, we met for a salon on the topic of emotional labor and life admin, inspired by two personally life-changing books: *Fed Up: Emotional Labor, Women, and the Way Forward* by Gemma Hartley and *Life Admin: How I Learned to Do Less, Do Better, and Live More* by Elizabeth Emens. Life admin is the unpaid work, from household chores to scheduling appointments to paying bills, that keeps your life on track. Emotional labor is tending to the emotional needs of those around you and can also be an umbrella term that includes life admin.

I was interested in the topic after connecting earlier that year with Elizabeth Emens through my work for the Southern Independent Booksellers Alliance. In an educational webinar we hosted, Emens spoke to booksellers on how they could reduce and redistribute life admin whenever possible, so they have more time to enjoy life and avoid burnout. Wouldn't we all want that? Although on the path to recovery in both realms, I was still doing the heavy lifting of life admin *and* emotional labor in different areas of my life, at the expense of creative play and much-needed rest. Reading these books offered me concrete ways to make big changes. I looked forward to talking about this subject at the salon because I was interested in sharing what I'd learned and finding out where others were in this realm of their lives. When I was coming up with ideas for the salon, I centered a quote by Audre Lorde: "I have come to believe that caring for myself is not self-indulgent. Caring for myself is an act of survival."

I began the day of the salon picking flowers to make posies for everyone as party favors, and ended it learning how each of us approached our lives' many tasks. I understood once more that the work to free ourselves of unnecessary patterns, and create liberating ones, never ends. We're still fighting gender roles; we need to examine the ways we contribute to our own servitude by putting ourselves last, because that's what so many women do.

During my interviews, a member explained the profound effect this salon had on her. "The emotional labor salon helped me understand the extent to which my life with my husband was out of balance, and brought my feelings of being deeply undervalued closer to the light. It made me confront how much I was the one doing the vast majority of the life admin work that is central, though it can seem invisible, to a family and household. My time, energy, and efforts were unpaid in every sense of the word, not by money, attention, or respect." This member has since gotten a divorce, though she and her husband remain friendly.

## The Afterglow of Salons: Emerging Themes and Patterns

I interviewed Lockie, a writer, radio show producer, and mover and shaker in our local community, at one of my favorite rooftop bars. The panoramic views of Asheville from this perch are stunning, especially at sunset, when the sky lights up with vibrant colors, and clouds cast shadows across the city streets and parks. Every time I drive downtown, I'm in awe of the city's special beauty, its architecture inspired by the art nouveau, beaux arts, art deco, and neo-Gothic traditions, nestled among the forest-covered Blue Ridge Mountains. Lockie and I were meeting late afternoon, at the end of my workday and before book club, which I host in the same venue. It was too cold to sit by the firepits outside, so we opted for a snug space inside by the bar.

Lockie has been in salon gatherings before ours, but she described them as more about artists and writers hanging out and networking than focused discussion. At this point in her life, she welcomed our salon's approach. She shared that she was "craving that opportunity to hear different points of view on a topic, and to reflect on how my opinions and views on the topic are changed and informed by what other people are saying. And so I welcomed that structure. It's so refreshing that the conversation is focused and is guided."

She has been struck by how often thoughts around the topics of our salons show up in other parts of her life, in casual conversations and activities. Doing the dishes with her husband prompted a discussion about our emotional labor salon and how as partners they navigated life admin. This particular theme especially resonated with her because of her age. She shared, "The theme of life admin is not only something that is ripe for the salon, but it is ripe for many of my friends. From empty nesters to freelance writers, the idea of life admin is something that affects all of us, yet I don't think I [was] thinking much about life admin when I was twenty-two and in my first apartment in San Francisco. It's the themes that you choose that seem like they are deeply topical for my friend groups at this point in our lives, so that we are already having these conversations, and I can add insights learned from the salon."

Another salon that turned out to be particularly timely for Lockie was "Reframing Regret," a deep dive into different forms of regret and how we address them and move on. She shared, "You were referencing a book and mentioned different types of regrets, including regrets of boldness. During the salon, we reflected on the different types of regrets, and it seems I did not have any regrets of boldness because I tend to dive headfirst in many areas of my life. The next day, I was talking to my friend who is a professor. She was talking about regrets, and it was clear that she was experiencing a regret of boldness. I told her my salon just explored this and explained the different types of regrets that I learned in the salon. She was really interested in the topic and said, "I love that phrase. Where did you get that information?" I was able to refer her to the author of the book and we continued discussing the other types of regrets. I gave her a framework for what she was feeling and a resource for her to explore through the book. More importantly, it helped her feel that she was not alone, and that I was not just listing my regrets in response to her regrets, but instead framing which [type] she was feeling and helping her name her feelings with more accuracy."

Lockie added, "The salon is very therapeutic for me during the actual salon meetings, as I explore my feelings with the group, but also afterwards, as I'm able to take those concepts into the broader world. Especially in the days following the salon, the themes filter into my other conversations and the insights gained influence how I walk in the world as I discover my own patterns."

## WIDENING YOUR FRIEND CIRCLE

I met Constance in a local "Eastern tearoom" with Bohemian roots; the network of tea shops of which this one is a part started in Prague during the last years of Communism. The tearoom is in a converted bank, where during the pandemic I opened a business account for the organization I work for. Once a visually dull place I associated with social distancing, masks, and hand sanitizer (applied after I used the bank's pens to sign documents), it's now a warm, welcoming space with a gas fireplace and cozy nooks for meeting on chairs, benches, or floor pillows. Asian art decorates the walls, and shelves of delicate tea sets are displayed near the counter where you place orders. It's one of the few restaurants in town where conversation doesn't compete with music, the perfect spot for our interview.

The tearoom serves an extensive menu of Chinese and thematic house-blended teas. Constance and I settled in with our choices (my go-to is their "vulnerabili-tea") near the fireplace. Constance is a children's book writer and illustrator whose wicked sense of humor and deep compassion moved us from critique partners to great friends. She is one of the salon's original members.

She shared that when the salon started, she was going through a dark time in her parenting journey. She had some initial misgivings about joining something that seemed so structured and sounded "like work more than a party." She was not looking for another chore. However, she was won over by what she called "a new experience, organized to achieve a certain goal and reflect on an issue together." She appreciated "the evolving deep conversation, and sharing in a way we don't do in normal life." When asked about what salons have added to her life, she said, "They are empowering and stay with me. I keep thinking about them." And for how they've affected her outside of the salons themselves, she brought up a theme that many members have shared—an unexpected widening of their friend circles. "Several of the women have become real friends who I see in other contexts such as lunch dates, movie outings, walks in nature. We've already established connections by being vulnerable, open, and exercising positive, active listening and communication in the salons, so connecting as friends beyond that feels natural."

# The Black Swans Share What Works

"These days, I'm looking for ways to slow the pace at which I live my life, to forge more meaningful relationships, and to broaden the scope through which I view the world. I appreciate that the salon, and its members, consistently support me in navigating these intentions."
—Clara, Black Swan Salon member

WHEN I INTERVIEWED MEMBERS OF my salon to hear their thoughts about our salon journey together, it was just before winter; the light lingered more briefly each day, and we began wearing sweaters and scarves to keep off the chill. I'd drive across town to their homes or meet them in cafés and tea shops, always hoping to return before dark, especially if I was driving over the mountains. When I met with Ryn at her log cabin in the woods, I decided to take the Blue Ridge Parkway home. It's a shortcut, and a route I prefer when possible because it offers breathtaking views of the mountains, a lower speed limit, and no stoplights. The way up to the parkway from Ryn's cabin is a paved two-lane that narrows to a single-file gravel road. It was almost sundown, and there were no streetlights, so I turned on my high beams as I approached the top, only to turn them off to take in the fading colors of a glorious sunset over the mountain peaks. I spotted a raven flying through the trees, going deeper into the woods, and glimpsed the white tails of deer as they leapt out of view. Because of the soul-deep conversation I'd just experienced, the moment felt primal, like the boom of a drum at the end of a powerful passage of music.

It's always so interesting, and a welcome pleasure, to see someone's home. I'm curious about their choice of colors for the walls, furniture and rugs, the way the light enters through windows and skylights, their taste in art, whether they feature family photos or keep that more private, if they trend minimalist or in the opposite direction, if a furry friend shares this space. How does the person who attends the salon, who has become my friend, feather their nest? One of the salon members took me into her bathroom to show how, influenced by our salons on the senses and sanctuary, she created a special setting for relaxation. She said, "Around the winter solstice, I bathe to soak the chill out of my bones, and when I do, I light several candles with polished silver and mirrors to reflect. I set up a tall tripod iron stand to hold an open candle in the corner and use a large crystal bowl to house my iPhone, which serves as an amplifier. I play medieval musical selections while I take an Epsom salt bath, sometimes with a special essential oil to add fragrance such as cedar or frankincense."

Almost seven years into hosting salons, I realize this is the first time I've delved into each member's experience of what it's like to attend them. They've let me know how much they love the salons in post-salon emails and texts—"They are just a wonderful respite" and "It's like a warm embrace"—but I wanted to understand more of the "why," the elements of the secret sauce we've cooked up together that make our salons so important to us. Most of the current members have been attending since the very beginning. We've gone from hardly knowing each other to knowing each other deeply. We've shared with vulnerability and trust our fears, hopes, regrets, and happy and difficult memories. Because of the newly added element of a clothing swap at the end of our salons, we're even wearing each other's clothes! These interviews revealed a number of recurring threads for hosts to bear in mind as their own salons evolve.

If you're considering forming or joining a salon (and I hope this book inspires you to do so!), you'll gain some good tips in this chapter to make them even better and retain, even grow if that is your goal, your membership. These interviews affirmed the best of what I was trying to do through our gatherings, and revealed areas where I can tweak or let go to improve for the future. The last decade has offered me many lessons, and among them are that communication, no matter what the issue, builds trust, compassionate leadership makes for great hosting, and dealing with problems as they arise avoids greater problems down the line.

## THE GOLDEN TICKET

When I first invited members to my salon, I sent the invitation by email. To my amazement, everyone accepted! The word that kept coming up when I asked in interviews how they felt when they received the invitation was "delighted." They also expressed being thrilled, intrigued, curious, elated, and inspired.

Most had never received an invitation to a group before and this touched them. They'd joined groups on their own, or started groups of one kind or another, but receiving a special invitation to a salon was memorable enough, seven years on, to bring a smile and comments like, "I fancied myself Anaïs Nin or Colette," "I imagined drawing rooms in Europe, and someone playing a pianoforte," and "It was like stepping into a Jane Austen novel!" I was surprised when they mentioned never (or hardly ever) receiving invitations to join groups, but then I reflected on that and realized it was true for me, as well. Once we leave high school or college, invites to exclusive groups are rare. This was something that I'd not given much weight to, but now I do, and I share here to emphasize that receiving an invitation to a salon can be like a golden ticket. It's truly special!

Treat your invitation like the precious thing it is. Consider including an actual golden ticket within a mailed/posted invitation to salon members. If I were to do this again, I would, at the very least, craft a beautiful evite or compose handwritten invitations on special cards. Remember that this might be the first time the folks you're inviting have been invited to anything like this, and that is a meaningful, cherished gift quite rare these days. In a culture where we crave connection, someone reaching out to us to say our presence is desired and valued can really lift our spirits.

## THE IMPORTANCE OF SAFE SPACES

"What I've noticed, having been in different circles for decades, is that they disintegrate when there isn't a container, when there isn't a structure and there aren't basic protocols which create mutual respect and emotional safety. In the groups where there is not mutual respect and emotional safety, people are harmed."

—Ryn, Black Swan Salon member

Another element that came up time and again for salon members was the importance of emotional safety. Even though I wasn't yet on the friend level with some of those invited, they knew me or other members and felt safe with us. The salon rules, which came with the invitation, included elements like confidentiality and respectful conversation, which also helped ease any concerns. One salon member shared, "Because I know you, I felt safe going into it. If I didn't feel safe, I wouldn't have gone in there. For me, what's really important is a salon being a safe, sacred space to really explore in." Another admitted that she was at first apprehensive, but went ahead and attended. After her first salon, she recalled, "I remember thinking this is a really caring, safe group of people." A newer member knew me through my bookselling days and exercise classes we'd attended together and shared, "Even though I had never had an intimate conversation with you, I felt I could trust you. . . . How could anyone who loved books and yoga and even Pilates not be trusted?"

My salon members also really liked that the salon was women-only. One said, "I might not have joined if men were involved." Another shared, "I was always happy that the salons are a women-only space, as I find it easier to be comfortable and open in the company of women."

It was my choice to be women-only because so much of my life had been under one male umbrella or another (this could be more broadly described as "the patriarchy"). I'd also been in physically and emotionally unsafe places with men (with women, too, but more intensely at risk with men) and felt safest opening up and being vulnerable with other women. This is admittedly a binary approach for specific reasons, including exploring many of the salon themes from the perspective of gender. We've discussed #MeToo, aging, beauty, emotional labor, strong women, and anger, for example, and in each case, we talked about how our gender influenced our relationship to the topic. As one member offered, "Although the perspectives of individual members vary, the fact that we're all women provides a shared experience that strengthens our connection to each other."

A salon can of course be mixed gender and a safe space. What I needed and what my members were drawn to is very specific to us and our lived experiences. However you define the qualities you are seeking in your members, when you create your own rules of engagement, concerns about respecting emotional safety can be explicitly stated, or implied within conversational ground rules like not interrupting, not judging, and honoring confidentiality. It's impossible to guarantee emotional safety because our triggers are so individual and sometimes not even known until the trigger occurs, but we can seek to support emotional safety in how we host and whom we choose to be part of our community.

## THE COMPANY YOU KEEP

"I remember meeting all these fabulous women and feeling 'undressed'—as in, insecure to be in the presence of such interesting women. I think my shyness is the most challenging part for me. Our salons are helping me feel less afraid to share my feelings."
—Black Swan Salon member

In an earlier chapter I mentioned the importance of care when selecting your members. Who was invited was entirely up to me, and although most of the members stayed with the salon after their first meeting, there were a few who self-selected out over time. One moved away, another had to focus on caring for a sick family member, another realized she was overstimulated by the group discussions, and another was more introverted than our format allowed for her to be comfortable. We've had members who didn't easily share space in conversation, and others who took several salons to become okay with opening up and being vulnerable. As host, I'm always scanning to see how members are relating to each other, and whether I need to step in and speak in the moment, or later, privately, to address any behavior that might not be desirable or appropriate for our group.

I recently heard this lyric from the song by Lyndsey Scott, *The Way Knows the Way*: "You don't have to know the way. The way knows the way." This has, for the most part, been my experience with the salon. Things generally sort themselves out; the way knows the way. The person who didn't share space in conversation no longer attends, the shyer folks are more comfortable opening up and speaking. But as one member mentioned while recalling negative experiences in other groups, "while the idea of a group is great, there's really a potential for toxic and controlling behavior because it's such a magnified relationship. A group dynamic magnifies things that are healthy or toxic." The extra care you take when selecting members will go a long way in avoiding behavior that can harm others in your group and work against your plans for the discussion. If you notice someone will not obey your rules of engagement, you have to nip it in the bud. A current salon member shared, "If someone goes off on a long tangent and 'hogs' the conversation, it not only feels wrong, it actually makes me anxious. I have such an urge to direct, that I want to tell people to follow the guidelines, share with an eye toward leaving enough time for others, and stay on topic." I address this specific problem more in our "Troubleshooting the Unexpected" chapter, but will remind hosts here that if someone's behavior makes you uncomfortable, it's likely making others even more uncomfortable, as they are not in the position, as non-hosts, to assert authority. Other important membership care elements to bear in mind:

  ⮞ Once you establish a core group, any new members may require vetting by the core group before becoming permanent members. A potential new member could be a "guest" for one session, and then the core group decides whether to let them become permanent members. In my interviews, I discovered that members develop a sense of ownership in the salon; they've evolved a relationship over time and built up a sense of trust, safety, and intimacy that can be threatened if a new person comes in. When adding members, consider this important step of vetting.

➤ If a member leaves the group permanently, or goes on sabbatical, let the others know that member's status. I'd underestimated how deeply bonded my salon was and how the unexplained absence of a member could cause unease (I thought they would know the reason, or that it wasn't so important; I was wrong on both counts). Share what you can, to the extent you respect confidentiality of the absent member.

## There Is Nothing Like This

"Your salons are different from any gathering I've experienced in the past."
—Constance, Black Swan Salon member

Gathering with intention, in a safe space where folks can feel comfortable being vulnerable, being heard, and speaking from the heart, is rare. Time and again, members shared that other gatherings, even if they had a goal, like a discussion of a certain book, often devolved into purely social time with random conversation.

One member writes about how our salon has changed over time: "I see a personal social evolution. And not just because of the questions that you present, and the topics, but because of what people share. The salon in and of itself is an enriching experience. It's very pleasurable. But I'm learning as we go along that the salon is really the catalyst for so much more. I mean, I enjoy the salon in itself. But the longer we go with this, the deeper the friendships form around it, the more we share, the more it enriches my life."

Words Black Swan members used to describe the salon: nourishing (most common descriptor!), challenging, engaging, fun, expansive, thought-provoking, laughter-filled, a place of wisdom, a celebration of vulnerability, safe, and (a personal favorite) "just a cool group of women getting together in a cozy home."

What does this mean for you? It means you can create or contribute to something unlike anything else happening in your life. Approach it with intention, respect, and joy, and be part of how it evolves. If you're the host, or doing this with a cohost or team, remember that one of the main aspects that sets your event apart from anything else is focused discussion on a topic. Don't stray too far from your salon's mission.

## THE TEACHING STORY

Every so often, a member shares a memory that will come up again and again because it's so unique and wise. Other members will refer to it, and with each retelling we learn a bit more about the lessons it offers. The story becomes a golden thread, woven into our shared salon journey. Consider noting this kind of story in your salon journal, should you keep one, as it might become the equivalent of a fast-growing mushroom, a rich topic you can build a salon around. Ryn's reflection on a swimming lesson with her grandmother serves this purpose for the Black Swan Salon. I asked her to share more for readers, so here is her story:

My paternal grandmother gave me my first swimming lesson. It was, hands down, the most influential life lesson I've ever received. The way I've lived my life since wouldn't be recognizable without it.

Grandma was a character. The family joke is that the roaring twenties ended when Grandma, who was five foot two with eyes of blue, married on July 3, 1930. Back then it was customary to marry on or during a holiday period for work-scheduling purposes. Knowing my grandparents, they probably picked July 3 so they could weave fireworks and parades with marching bands into their wedding nuptials. Grandma, or Ginny as she was called, often donned a red beret and always wore bright red nail polish and clip-on earrings. Her signature scent was Taboo. My grandfather was her driving instructor, which is how they met, and she took great pride in her driving skills. She loved to speed, and bribed the local police department with her brownies. She never received a speeding ticket and smiled and waved at the officers as she sped by them.

Grandma was attracted to mysteries of the sacred, like palmistry and tea leaves. Because she was a Cancer and I am a Pisces, with five planets in water signs, she was very interested in my relationship with water. One summer when I was seven, she asked me about swimming. I told her I wanted to learn, but no one would teach me. She frowned and I could sense she was really biting her tongue. As we prepared to go together to the pool, she went on and on about how amazing the Olympic speed swimmer Mark Spitz was. Clearly, she was enamored, and as I stated, speedy movement was a thrilling aspect of life for her. She wondered aloud why some people could swim more quickly than others. She deduced it was a matter of strong faith expressed in trust for the water along with a clear sense of direction, strength, and flexibility.

When we got to the pool, she said the first step in learning how to swim was learning how to float. To learn how to float, you have to have faith that the water will hold you, and trust in that faith. Otherwise, if you panic, or lose faith in water, you could drown.

Next, she asked if I trusted her to hold me while I lay face up on the water. I assured her I trusted her completely. She put both her arms out to support me, and I laid back in the water while she coached me to breathe and relax.

After we practiced this a couple of times, she shared that she was old and her arms were tired of holding me up, but the water would never tire of holding me up.

Did I trust the water to hold me? 'Oh, yes, Grandma!' I replied, and then she encouraged me to float without her arms under my back.

To my amazement, I did NOT float! I was shocked because surely I had the faith to float! Almost immediately, my feet started to sink, and I began flailing my arms. She said, 'I thought you trusted the water?' 'I do, Grandma!' I said, confused. She urged me to try again with more patience and calm. Once again, my feet slowly sank. I started to kick my feet and swing out my arms to stay above water, which made things worse. However, I kept trying and began to observe the difference between being tense or calm in my body. With patient practice, I was soon floating on my own.

Before we left the pool, she looked deeply into my eyes and said to remember this, that when I became a woman, it was very important to exercise this kind of faith when it came to loving a man, and also for moving through life. Keep faith, have direction, keep patience, and be strong. She added, with enough faith, I could be shipwrecked in the middle of the ocean, and the water would bring me to shore. If you keep faith, you'll float; if you panic, you could drown. Always remember to keep faith!

## Consider a Salon Journal

Several salon members mentioned using, or wanting to use, a journal to write about the salon-related work they were doing on their own. One mused, "I really wish I kept a salon notebook. When I get a wild hair, I decide I'm going to go through that pile of unfiled papers. I've been so happy when I've come across a sheet from a salon that triggers memories. I wish I had a special folder for our salons or a journal with pockets."

I'm a fervent bullet journal (aka BuJo) enthusiast, and as much as I love journaling, I hadn't thought to formally introduce this element into my salon. It really makes sense though, as salons are often just the beginning of our relationship with a theme. We are urged through the discussion at the salon, through questionnaires I hand out, through the quotes we share, to dig deeper.

A salon notebook can also function as a dream journal if you want to keep all your reflections in one place, and especially if your salon journey inspires your dreams. One member, Constance, let me know that after our salon on dreams, she started a dream journal. "The dreams salon was SO fascinating! I listened in wonder as the women around me recounted their dreams that were often similar to mine, contained repeated motifs, and were also very specific to each individual—and revealed so much. I saw how deeply and richly some people experience their dream/unconscious/subconscious realities. It strengthened my sense of the awesomeness of our subconscious life and inspired me to start a dream journal. Though I only record my dreams sporadically, it's still been an interesting endeavor and a direct result of that salon."

What kind of journal you opt for is a personal choice, and you may discover that your initial choice isn't the best. If you choose something that turns out not to be to your liking, just go ahead and get one that does work for you. Don't be a journal martyr. I've been there and I have several barely written-in journals in my bookcase to prove it.

From my experience as a journaler, and as a bookseller who used to engage with customers in long conversations about them at our bookstore, I advise you to choose what calls to you and matches your overall "style." Journals can be beautiful art objects with gorgeous covers, or they can be minimalist, like the Leuchtturm1917 brand monochromatic bullet journals I prefer (though I decorate their pages with my drawings).

OTHER THINGS TO CONSIDER WHEN CHOOSING YOUR JOURNAL:
> **Paper quality.** Make sure the inside paper is of excellent quality and writing won't bleed through to the other side of a page. This kind of paper is sometimes called "ink proof" as it has a special coating that can handle even fountain pen ink without bleeding. If purchasing at a bookstore, ask the

bookseller about the paper quality, as they'll likely know or can find out for you through a bit of research.

> **Binding.** Sewn-in pages, as opposed to glued pages, will stay much longer in their binding. A spiral binding is great for artwork but isn't the best choice for journaling: The spiral binding can work its way out of the notebook, and is cumbersome and easily damaged when fitting into a satchel or backpack. Look for a "lay flat" binding, often indicated in the journal description on the cover or just inside; it's easier to write in. Try laying the journal flat. Does it resist you? Does it seem like the pages will come loose and the binding crack? If so, don't get this journal. If you're in the store testing this out with a journal, be gentle when opening and don't damage it.

> **Pockets.** Choose a journal with pockets inside the binding. Trust me, you'll be glad you did! If your salon has handouts, like mine, you can stow them in the pockets, along with any other mementos, like the letter you wrote to your future self on goals.

> **Page format.** What do you plan to do with your journal? What style makes that easiest for you? Do you want blank, lined, grid, or dotted? I prefer dotted because I write and draw and use my journal as a day planner, but if you are simply writing, perhaps another style works best to support that intention.

> **Size.** Does the journal size work well for how you're going to store it in your backpack, pocketbook, bookcase, or on your desk or bedside night table?

# SALON STARTER KITS & ENCOURAGEMENT

# Fourteen Themed Salon Starter Kits

"Seek out what magnifies your spirit. . . . Who are the people, ideas, and books that magnify your spirit? Find them, hold on to them, and visit them often."
—Maria Popova

These salon starter kits come directly from the Black Swan Salon. They provide templates and resources to get you started and save you time while you focus on other aspects of the gathering. You can use them as is, add or subtract elements depending on the length and goals of your gathering, or simply use them as general inspiration for approaching topics more relevant to what you'd like to explore with your salon.

The elements for each template include:

> - Salon description: use with your invite or social media event post
> - Prep email: sent (or mailed or posted on social media) before the salon
> - Teaser & enricher: a way to personalize and enrich the salon
> - Personal backstory: often the inspiration for the salon theme
> - Salon questionnaire: for members to fill out before the general discussion and take home; this exercise preps them for the discussion
> - Breakout questions: for small group discussions
> - Large group questions: for discussion by the entire salon
> - Closing: reflection on the salon experience
> - Thematic quotes: members read aloud at the end of the salon

I alternate salon topics from heavier themes, like #MeToo and aging, to potentially lighter ones, like beauty and fashion. I use the word "potentially" because in our salon the conversation still goes quite deep; these subjects touch different parts of our histories and personalities and intersect with our bodies and our emotional and financial resources. No matter what the topic, be sensitive to what might come up. Also, give some thought to how you might thread the flow of themes you choose, as one topic can build upon another, though all can function as stand-alones.

For each starter kit, I provide the inspiration and a bit of personal backstory. In some cases, my thoughts reflect an issue I was grappling with and have since resolved. They may resonate with where you and your salon are on your timelines. I encourage you to substitute your own backstory, or feel free to share along with mine, as your group will always appreciate learning about *your* unique experiences. We're all on a journey, and hearing from fellow travelers makes us feel less alone. Although it can seem risky to share your private concerns and personal history in front of others, some of whom you might not know very well, I've never regretted it, especially if confidentiality is one of the ground rules. By opening up, you encourage others to do the same.

I also share, where it might be helpful for hosts, our salon's experience with the theme, to give you a heads up on some issues that might arise for members. Every salon brings unexpected conversations; you'll find yourself back on your heels at times, but these moments can change your perspective, shift you into a new level of relationship with someone, and stay with you long after you close the salon session. And if it was awkward, lesson learned!

## FASHION

Our salon on fashion was one of our most popular, and it's a subject I keep thinking about. I was at a tea shop, waiting for a friend to arrive, and opted to discreetly people-watch instead of turning to my phone. I was struck by how artfully the other patrons were dressed. A lot of athleisure, leggings, or body-skimming skirts and pants, complemented by soft sweaters and fleece with rolled hems at the wrist, waist, or neck. The look was creative, flattering, intriguing, timeless. Reminiscent of Eileen Fisher, but more youthful and form-fitting, more daring in the cut of the cloth and the design and structure of the garments. I was wearing a very conventional outfit: jeans, button-down tailored blouse, and wrap sweater. Nice, but hardly memorable or artistic. I realized I felt kind of frumpy. When I got home, I looked at the closet I've purged countless times, still tight with clothes. I wondered, if I lost it all and had to rebuild my wardrobe, would I choose any of what's in there? After staring, uninspired, at my smushed clothes on hangers, I actually left my bedroom and googled, "Is my wardrobe holding me back?"

Instead of purchasing a whole new wardrobe, as the online world suggested, I decided to make a little more effort to style myself with what I already had, trying out new combinations of items and colors to be a bit more playful, prioritizing garments that pop or subtly complement. I packed up what I wasn't using regularly, like the dresses and sweaters I never reached for when there was an opportunity to wear them; it was time for the next person to enjoy them. Anything worn-looking, with faded colors, small holes, or pilling, was discarded. Now I have some room to purchase a new item or two if I need an update, and I can see my remaining clothes more easily. I'm not pretending this was easy to do, because I was invested, financially and sentimentally, in many of the items I gave away, but my remaining clothes appreciate the breathing room, and I'm having more fun choosing what to wear each day.

At our fashion salon, the economic differences between members suddenly became clearer, especially when our discussion turned to the topic of favorite designers. One member later told me, "A lot came up for me about entitlement, feeling unworthy of 'nice' things, always feeling compelled to shop 'sale only,' class issues, etc. One of the wealthier women was talking about her 'favorite designers' and I felt very alienated by that—her life experience is so different from mine. As if I could have a favorite designer! Maybe a favorite rack at the Belk outlet store." This member shared that the discussion reminded her of how her family had shopped for clothes on sale out of necessity; she recalled her mother's response whenever someone complimented her on her outfits, proudly declaring a variation on: "It was originally twenty-five dollars, but I got it for seven!" Her recollections reminded me that my family, too, shopped sale only at discount stores. Well into adulthood, whenever I visited my mother, she'd take me to thrift stores, or "boutiques," as she called them. I often discovered great vintage finds among the racks of baggy clothing smelling faintly of mothballs and cigarettes. But these shopping dates increasingly wore at me; I felt trapped in a cycle of poverty, reminded that I could rarely afford to purchase new clothing, and was instead trying on tired-looking garments in dingy dressing rooms, with seventies "classics" blaring over the stereo system.

This member reckoned with her frustration around her limitations, but also valued the openness with which people shared, and was glad for the conversation. It's just hard sometimes, and that's part of what comes with salons: being uncomfortable and dealing with it, as well as noticing discomfort in others and appreciating their struggle. Other members came away with a new awareness of their privilege, along with thoughts like, "What am I saying with what I'm wearing? What do my clothes say about me?"

### Salon Description
Fashion is wearable art, a means of self-expression, a way to develop and evince a personal style. How we respond to fashion, play with it, rebel against it, ignore it, and change with it as we mature will make for a wonderful conversation. Let's talk about it!

### Prep Email
I don't know about you all, but I've been putting more effort into new combinations of clothing I already own, and wearing jewelry, which I often skip. It takes just a moment's thought and yet my husband keeps saying, "You look nice!" and I'm

thinking, "I'm barely trying, but thank you!" I was likely in a pandemic survival rut; I'd set the bar so low on self-presentation that anything above sweats and a messy hair bun now knocks it out of the park. I'll be curious to hear if thinking about the theme has also affected your fashion awareness.

## Teaser & Enricher

At our salon gathering, wear clothes that represent your fashion sense now or in the past. You could wear your favorite fashion of all time (could be from any era, including before you were born), or make an anti-fashion statement (which is, of course, a fashion statement). We'll take a photo at the salon to memorialize the gathering.

## Personal Backstory Shared at Salon

I passively take in fashion when I'm online and out and about. I note how we present ourselves through our clothing, jewelry, hairstyle, and makeup choices. Some of us voice an indifference to fashion, others, an obsession. My passion around fashion is situational, but I'm firmly in the fashion is art camp and supportive of personal expression, however outlandish or ephemeral it might seem to others. Humans are fascinating, and part of what sets us apart from other animals is our fashion.

I've been making more conscious fashion choices lately and observing where I'm going with things like hem lengths, jean styles, and heel height. I'm looking anew at colors and patterns, mulling how they amplify or mute my mood. When shopping for a few outfits to wear to a wedding in Cancún, I found myself in the juniors' department at Dillard's because the clothing for adults was so BORING. The kids had all the fun stuff! So, it was me and a couple of teens looking at ourselves in the mirror in the dressing room. I wonder what they thought of me wearing clothes that were designed with them in mind. Were my choices, by default because of my age, "uncool" or did I have a special status? I don't know, as they gave me nothing expression-wise. But when I wore one of my juniors' outfits to the wedding reception, a young waitstaff at the bar gave me a thumbs up, and I felt great.

**Salon Questionnaire**

➢ Quick: What words come to mind when you think of the word *fashion*?

➢ On a scale of 1–10, with 10 being the highest, how does your physical presentation of yourself reflect the inner you?

➢ Is clothing a utilitarian choice for you or a form of creative expression?

➢ Do finances play a role in your fashion? If money were no object, what might you do differently?

➢ Do you have a favorite designer or two? Who are they and why do you love them?

➢ Has your fashion sense or personal style evolved over time or is it pretty set?

**Breakouts: Questions for Discussion**

➢ Is there a specific item (shoes, socks, undergarments, tops, pants, dresses, scarves, jewelry, coats) that you tend to focus more thought on when purchasing and/or deciding how to dress for the day?

➢ Why do you think that is?

➢ Is there a favorite fashion style (preppy, Victorian, grunge, athleisure, boho, classic, minimalist, gender-fluid, etc.) or element (big shoulder pads, skinny or flared jeans, track-suit, flowy dress, platform shoes) that you have special fondness for?

➢ Any that you really don't like?

➢ When growing up, did you notice your parents' or other caretaker's fashion sense?

➢ Can you describe it? Did it influence you?

**Large Group Questions**

➢ How do you view fashion in a discussion of feminism?

➢ Do you have any fashion or anti-fashion role models or designers?

➢ How often do you assess your wardrobe and purge items?

➢ Do you shop often or only when you need to replace something?

➢ Do finances play a role in your fashion choices? If money were no object, what might you do differently?

## Closing
While clothing is one of our basic needs for survival, along with food and shelter, it can also be a form of self-expression and wearable art. But it needn't be. What is on our bodies is entirely our business. In our salon we ranged in approaches from highly practical to very whimsical, from sensual to quite modest. I've been thinking about what I am saying and projecting through what I'm wearing, and whether this is a conscious choice, or someone else's choice, or me being lazy. Some of us have been so influenced by family and societal pressures that we've never made our own choices around fashion. Isn't it about time to start?

## Quotes Selected by Salon Members
"Fashion you can buy, but style you possess. The key to style is learning who you are, which takes years. There's no how-to road map to style." —Iris Apfel

"Fashion is the armor to survive the reality of everyday life." —Bill Cunningham

"Fashion is very important. It is life-enhancing and, like everything that gives pleasure, it is worth doing well." —Vivienne Westwood

"Fashion should be a form of escapism, and not a form of imprisonment." —Alexander McQueen

"You can have whatever you want in life if you dress for it." —Edith Head

"Reinvent new combinations of what you already own. Improvise. Become more creative. Not because you have to, but because you want to. Evolution is the secret for the next step." —Karl Lagerfeld

### EMOTIONAL LABOR: OWNING OUR WORTH

I'm going to share a little story about Edith Bunker and me and how I escaped a pattern. My mother was just like Edith Bunker, a character in the seventies sitcom *All in the Family*. My father was not Archie Bunker, Edith's husband, but he accepted my mom being Edith. He worked at an office, and she managed all home chores. She did all the cooking, she did all the housework. He contributed around the house on weekends, but generally, it was her realm. Mom would run around the house serving him. She was slavish to a disturbing degree. She would be coy and mispronounce words on purpose, and it embarrassed me. But she was a woman of her time. Smart and talented, yet isolated in her home as she didn't drive until her forties, nor do I remember her being encouraged to. I vowed I would not be her.

But I became Edith! The adult me morphed into a martyr, rescuer, doormat, and overall "one who endures." To borrow from Virginia Woolf, I became the Angel in the House, self-sacrificing my dreams to domesticity. I tucked those dreams away while trying to make the life I had work. But the narrative I was constantly rewriting to turn into a happy story could not overcome the reality of how miserable it all was. Eventually, and somewhat dramatically, it all came crashing down. I'm now a recovered Edith, with endless compassion and admiration for my mother, who eventually shed being Edith and began to assert herself in her final decades. Including learning to drive, which was actually kind of terrifying if you were a passenger (her barking "Gun it!" while taking rashly considered left turns will forever stay with me), but good for her, anyway! When I remarried, I started to fall back into former patterns and my husband called me out on it, gently but persistently. I now "let" him do things for me, and sometimes I drop the ball on purpose so he can pick it up. We're both givers; if anything, we have to work against our own compulsions to do for the other, and accept being taken care of. This is not a bad problem to have, really. Now I'm finding time to follow some dreams, and he is super supportive.

Our salon on emotional labor really resonated with members, sparking conversations with their families about more fairly delegating and outsourcing household tasks. A few of us became accountability partners for each other, to offer support when we took on tasks we hated but couldn't avoid, like tax prep and paying bills. I felt a greater appreciation for all the life admin I accomplish, but I resolved to lighten my load. After this salon, I hired housecleaning services, which is one of the best gifts I've ever given to myself.

**Salon Description**
Emotional labor, also called "life admin," is the unpaid work that goes into keeping those around you, or in a relationship with you, comfortable and happy. It ranges from doing household chores to paying bills and taxes, feeding everyone, and scheduling appointments. These tasks are a necessary part of adult life, but are you taking care of yourself and not taking on more than you should for others? If you have a full-time job outside the home, adding on the emotional labor of dealing with all the needs of family members can take up time we could otherwise use for moving important personal goals forward and supporting our mental and physical health. Can we assess what we're doing, share the burden of these efforts with those around us, and find time for joy and relaxation? Can we make sure that we're not spending too much time admin-ing and not living? Let's talk about emotional labor and share tips and tricks on celebrating and offloading it.

**Prep Email**
This year I've read three books on the subject of emotional labor: *Life Admin: How I Learned to Do Less, Do Better, and Live More* by Elizabeth Emens, *Fed Up: Emotional Labor, Women, and the Way Forward* by Gemma Hartley, and *Why We Can't Sleep: Women's New Midlife Crisis* by Ada Calhoun. Although men certainly can take on emotional labor, it disproportionately affects women. Many women are experiencing burnout, thinking it's caused by their professional work, when

it might instead (or also) be the time spent performing the emotional labor required to keep their personal lives (which might involve multiple people) in good order. The first step in recovery can be identifying the emotional labor in your life and then deciding how you want to handle it going forward. Consider whether you have found a healthy approach to it, negotiating with others to lighten the load, or even saying no at times, because it isn't how you want to spend your energy and time. Or is this an area of your life you need to pay more attention to so that you're taking better care of yourself?

### Teaser & Enricher:

Complete this at home before the salon:

> What is your life admin personality? Take this quiz (it's short and you'll like it): riddle.com/view/467549?qzzr=1.

> Where are you on the Wheel of Consent by Dr. Betty Martin? Download a copy of the Wheel of Consent at schoolofconsent.org/downloads.

### Personal Backstory Shared at Salon

So much of how we move in the world is reflected in our approach to emotional labor, and the extent it takes up space in our thoughts and on our schedules. I've been examining where I am in Dr. Martin's "Wheel of Consent." Too often I've inhabited the shadow sides of "serve" and "allow," and not accepted or even seen the possibility of help from others. I'm not blameless in how these patterns emerged; I've been my own worst enemy at times, willingly and naively slipping into roles that harmed my sense of self-worth, when I now wish I'd pushed back or walked away.

Happily, my relationship with emotional labor has evolved, helping to spark big shifts in relationships, jobs, and living situations. I've moved to the healthier areas of the wheel of consent and laid down some good boundaries. I outsource what I can take off my plate. I embrace the parts of me that enjoy life admin tasks, as ticking off the boxes on my to-do lists helps me feel more in control of my schedule and time.

## Salon Questionnaire
- On a scale of 1-5, with 5 being the most stressful, rate your emotional labor workload.
- If you could outsource any tasks, which would make the greatest difference to your quality of life?
- Are there any tasks you enjoy and feel proud of doing well? What are they?
- Do you feel guilty asking for help or delegating work to another family member? If yes, why do you think that is?
- If someone helps you, are you critical of their work? This happens, especially if you tend to take on a martyr role. Be honest.
- Do you ever discuss your emotional labor with anyone? Who?

## Breakouts: Questions for Discussion
- If you could take one or two things off your to-do list, what would they be?
- How would you do this? Who would help you? Could you outsource them?
- Have you ever taken on emotional labor to avoid difficult conversations? Discuss.
- How do you think other people perceive you in relation to emotional labor? Skilled? Challenged? How do you see yourself?

## Large Group Questions
- Do you ever suffer from what author Elizabeth Emens calls "madmin mind," when your mind is overwhelmed with admin concerns and tasks? What do you do to deal with this?
- What tools (apps, online calendars, bullet journals) do you use to help plan and delegate emotional labor's admin tasks?
- Do you ever talk about emotional labor with your partner, siblings, or children?
- Is emotional labor a feminist issue?

## Closing
A lot probably came up for you in this salon. A lot came up

for me when planning it. Here are a few things you might try to get started on taking back your life: Enlist an accountability partner to meet you in a café or on Zoom while you do something you really don't enjoy, like taxes, responding to emails, or creating a budget for a project. Consider, if you can afford it, paying someone to do those things you hate to do and take up precious time, like mowing the lawn, housecleaning, or grocery deliveries. If you're partnered and doing more than your share of the admin, or you're a slacker and guiltily aware you need to do more, have a conversation with your partner about ways to share the load more evenly. You got this.

### Quotes Selected by Salon Members

"I have come to believe that caring for myself is not self-indulgent. Caring for myself is an act of survival." —Audre Lorde

"Behind every working woman is an enormous pile of unwashed laundry." —Barbara Dale

"In politics, if you want anything said, ask a man. If you want anything done, ask a woman." —Margaret Thatcher

"I want the term 'gold digger' to include dudes who look for a woman who will do tons of emotional labor for them." —Erin Rodgers

"When the well's dry, we know the worth of the water." —Benjamin Franklin

"Love yourself first and everything else falls in line." —Lucille Ball

## On Friendship

The idea for this salon theme sprang from a conversation over dinner with the British philosopher A. C. Grayling when he was visiting our bookstore to promote and speak about his then newest book, *The God Argument: The Case Against Religion and For Humanism.* He was working on what would be his next book, *Friendship,* about types of friendship. This is a subject I think about often and discuss in another chapter, "An Example." Friendships can outlast romantic partnerships and even family. They are relationships we choose to bring into our lives, and they help us navigate loneliness and grief, allow us to share life's celebrations and simple events, and sometimes blossom into roommate and even romantic partnerships. As we know from so much research on loneliness, healthy friendships can, in truth, save us from despair and an early death.

Friendship is a rich topic for conversation, as our salon experienced. We spent the small group breakouts reflecting on childhood friendships, and the larger group session discussing adult friendships. Talking about a lifetime of friendships brought back many memories and revealed patterns in how we approach and value these relationships. We considered what we wanted in our friendships today and resolved to be more accepting and forgiving in these relationships, reminded through our discussion that one person can't be all things to us, nor should they be. But they can bring so much joy and companionship in their own ways.

### Salon Description

Much is written about the many forms and purposes of friendships in our lives. From soul friends to purely social friends, these connections enrich (and sometimes complicate) our lives, and can be more significant than romantic and familial relationships. Let's discuss our views on friendships and how we approach and tend to them.

**Prep Email**

This salon will be a deep dive on friendship. Friendships take many forms (platonic and romantic), serve a specific purpose, evolve, end, or become a constant presence. They may mean one thing to one friend, and another to the other. The idea of friendship has been a field of study since ancient times. Let's discuss what friendship means to us.

**Teaser & Enricher**

Do you have a favorite photo of you and a friend (could be a sibling)? A precious gift from them that you've always kept? If possible, bring these to the salon to display in an altar to friendship we'll set up for the duration of our time together.

**Personal Backstory Shared at Salon**

According to Aristotle, there are three kinds of friendship: friendships of utility, friendships of pleasure, and friendships of the good. Friendships of utility are friendships of mutual usefulness, like the person who fixes your computer in return for payment, or your neighbor, who agrees to get your mail while you're away, and you do the same for them. Friendships of pleasure are friendships centered around shared activities and interests, like friends with benefits, friends we socialize with, and friends with whom we share a specific hobby or passion in common, like hiking or playing music. Friendships of the good are more exalted. These are friendships based upon respect and appreciation for each other's qualities, not for the ways they are like you, or for the things they can do for you.

There are many other definitions of friend types, which can be variations on those three: best friends, social friends, situational friends, work friends, lifelong friends, and life-stage friends (friends with whom you might share a season or two as you go through something). And then there are the "friends" to avoid: one-sided friendships, codependent friends, toxic friends (the drama and chaos they bring sucks away your will to live; they are like the dementors in *Harry Potter*), and fake friends (ugh).

We don't need a friend to be all things, the way we can't expect a partner to be all things. I've also come to understand the importance of disentangling myself from toxic friendships. My therapist has said to me a few times, in a firm voice, "That person is NOT your friend." I have sobbed, I mean those body-wracking sobs, over the realization that a friendship meant more to me than to the other person, or when, and this could be the same person, I was totally deluded around what I perceived our friendship to be (that person was NOT my friend). My grief and anguish over instances like this has been deep. But leaving the toxicity and drama behind has meant that my present life is so much better.

I'm sure I annoy my current friends, and they might annoy me, but these are small annoyances that can be quite funny in the big scheme of things. We've laughed at the ways we are different and how our edges inadvertently poke at each other, catching ourselves bickering like younger versions of the Golden Girls. An immature trait I had as a younger person was abandoning my girlfriends when I entered into a romantic relationship with a man. I vowed not to do this when I started dating my husband.

## Salon Questionnaire

> According to Aristotle, there are three kinds of friendship: friendships of utility (mutual usefulness), friendships of pleasure (shared interests and activities), and friendships of the good (friendship based on respect and appreciation). Do you tend to have one form of friendship over the others?
> What is the age range of your friends? Mostly your age? Mostly younger or older? Multigenerational?
> Do you make regular friend dates?
> Do any of your family members also rate as friends?

## Breakouts: Questions for Discussion

> Did you have a special friend (could be a sibling) as a child?
> Describe their personality in three words.

➢ Do you have a fond memory of something you two did together—once or as a continuing activity?
➢ Are you still friends who keep in touch?
➢ Share if you've had or have a friend from a different culture or even country. How did you become friends?

## Large Group Questions

➢ Share traits that are especially important to you in adult friendships. And share if you have friends for different purposes, or tend to have a friend or two who does it all for you.
➢ We often have friends who are like us. Do you have any friends who push you to look at the world differently, friends who are windows, as opposed to mirrors? These could be friends from another country, culture, ethnicity, economic class, political ideology, spiritual path, gender, generation, etc.
➢ There is this intriguing idea of a romantic friendship, in which friends, usually of the same sex but not always, are physically affectionate, sometimes even sleeping in the same bed. They offer each other emotional support and companionship. Some say this term was used as cover for gay and lesbian couples of the past who didn't want to identify that way, or whom historians didn't want to identify that way. Have any of you had romantic friendships? Can you share briefly how your friendship developed and what place it serves in your life now?
➢ Do you seek out new friends, or are you content with those you have, and perhaps let new friends come to you?

## Closing

Our country is experiencing a loneliness epidemic, worsened by our experiences of isolation during and after the Covid era. Vivek H. Murthy, MD, former surgeon general of the United States, writes about the importance of friendship, and friendship circles, in his book, *Together: The Healing Power of Human Connection in a Sometimes Lonely World*. For so many adults, keeping and developing friendships can be daunting when work and family responsibilities take up our time and energy. And, as we learned in this salon, we might also put too much burden on our friends to be all things to us, rather than being grateful for whatever they do bring, be it simply taking in our garbage cans or checking our mail when we're away, or being our hiking partner or the person we can count on to go to the newest movie. Dr. Murthy writes about being gentle and forgiving and kind in our friendships: "Friendship needs to be tended with kindness. This kindness requires openhearted care and trust, empathy and honesty, and a generous dose of understanding so the connection can flourish and endure." He adds, "A profound side effect of friendship is gratitude. Gratitude for the opportunity to show vulnerability and still be loved. For the forgiveness of our flawed lives. For the shared trust and time together and the feeling of belonging, which is the ultimate glue that holds friends together."

## Quotes Selected by Salon Members

"It's the friends you can call up at 4 a.m. that matter."
—Marlene Dietrich

"A single rose can be my garden; a single friend, my world." —Leo Buscaglia

"Each friend represents a world in us, a world possibly not born until they arrive, and it is only by this meeting that a new world is born." —Anaïs Nin

"Let us be grateful to the people who make us happy; they are the charming gardeners who make our souls blossom." —Marcel Proust

"Things are never quite as scary when you've got a best friend." —Bill Watterson

"And a youth said, Speak to us of Friendship. And he answered, saying: Your friend is your needs answered." —Kahlil Gibran

## Embracing Vulnerability: Leaning In, Taking Risks

This salon arose after reading about vulnerability, especially as explored in the work of Brené Brown in her book *Daring Greatly*. I'd previously associated vulnerability with weakness, those places where we can be wounded, but she offers a way of looking at vulnerability as a positive quality, writing, "Vulnerability is the birthplace of innovation, creativity and change." This salon was one of our most personally revealing and inspiring. Watching salon members as they shared stories of facing their fears and embracing their vulnerabilities brought to mind kintsugi, the Japanese art of putting a broken object back together by joining the pieces with gold lacquer. Kintsugi's philosophy is "more beautiful for having been broken," as the repaired object is considered more lovely than the original. Not that any of us were broken—though perhaps during those stretches when we were in the midst of some particularly bad experience, we felt that way—but the ways we mended and tended to ourselves marked our spirits in ways that made us more beautiful, too, and certainly more compassionate and emotionally rich beings.

### Salon Description

Let's explore our attitudes toward vulnerability. For many of us, being vulnerable, in a place of uncertainty and emotional risk, brings up difficult emotions, including deep uneasiness, even panic. What makes you feel vulnerable? How do you deal with these moments? Do you, as author Susan Jeffers would say, "feel the fear and do it anyway"? Try to avoid putting yourself in these situations? Depends on context? Let's talk about it.

### Prep Email

When reading Rebecca Solnit's *A Field Guide to Getting Lost*, which turned out to be a perfect read before our salon, I came across a passage that touches on this topic: "Leave the door open for the unknown, the door into the dark. That's where the most important things come from, where you yourself came from, and where you will go." Our attitudes toward different kinds of vulnerability can move us forward or hold us back. Think about a significant time in your life when how you dealt with vulnerability became a turning point.

## Teaser & Enricher
Commit to doing something that scares you. Not something unsafe, of course, but something that brings up feelings of vulnerability. I took a belly dancing class at age fifty and performed in a public recital in front of a cheering crowd of mostly strangers. When I heard about the recital piece, requested of my belly dancing class by our teacher, I balked. Then an older member of the class said to me, "When you're seventy, wouldn't you regret not having done it?" She convinced me, and I'm so glad I put myself out there. The recital was exhilarating, liberating, and fun. Challenge yourself.

## Personal Backstory Shared at Salon
The definition of *vulnerable* according to Merriam-Webster is "1 : capable of being physically or emotionally wounded" or "2 : open to attack or damage : assailable."

In my readings this year, I've come across the perspective of looking at vulnerability as a positive quality. You don't wait for perfect timing or expect perfection in your work. Instead, you put yourself out there, you dive in, you're brave.

In my current thinking, to be vulnerable is to be open-hearted and unguarded, despite the emotional risk. If I'm feeling vulnerable, this tells me I'm stepping out of my comfort zone, which keeps me growing. In the past, my vulnerability, coupled with what I call "empathy without borders" and a strong sense of loyalty and commitment, became the setup for a train wreck, or three. I survived them and am much better off now because I resolved to become a better steward of my life.

I used to associate vulnerability with weakness, like the Merriam-Webster definition, "being open to attack or damage." Up until I succumbed to nervous exhaustion while dealing with a relative experiencing a prolonged psychotic episode,

I believed I was emotionally invulnerable. I would tell people that no matter what came at me, I could handle it. I was almost prideful about this. I was not invulnerable, of course, but what I was, absolutely, was *emotionally disconnected*. I put up shields to protect myself, I would tell people I was "fine," but inside I was crumbling. Nervous exhaustion became the tipping point and sparked the first great shift forward in my adult life.

In the wake of that experience, I decided I would work on facing, and even appreciating, my vulnerabilities. At the same time, I vowed to never refrain from doing something just because I was afraid. I was tired of being fearful. I didn't like that feeling in my body, and I still don't, though it arises and always will. Although I saw myself at that time as broken, I pushed myself to be more daring. I became more compassionate toward other emotionally vulnerable people. I recognized myself in their struggles; I grew.

A more recent time of vulnerability was leaving a job I'd worked at for many years and had connected very deeply with my sense of self and purpose. I realized it was time to seek out new opportunities and challenges, a new work horizon. During this transition—finding a new job, giving notice, and serving out the final weeks at my position—I felt very vulnerable, in the sense of uncomfortable, scared, uncertain, living in that "not knowing" state, about so much. I literally cried and sweated this decision; I don't think I've felt so vulnerable outside of my divorce. Yet, this change has been one of the best things I've done for myself. I'm now in the healthiest place I've been, possibly ever, in my life. It's kind of astonishing, actually.

You can find inspiration for embracing risk and vulnerability everywhere, if you're open to it. Ever since I heard author Kwame Alexander tell a crowd of booksellers that he responded "Yes!" to everything and figured out the details later, I've begun saying yes to every opportunity that shows promise and feels like something I can manage, either on my own or with help, without being overwhelmed. I have not once regretted it.

What does being vulnerable feel like to me now? If I'm not in a good space, it can still feel unsettling, even scary. I get snappish, I doubt myself, I doubt others, I get ridiculously obsessed with "order" about the house and in my work. The voice in my head is very judgmental. But when I'm in a good space, which is most often, vulnerable feels like promise, hope, being alive, experiencing the depths of emotion without shields. I'm engaged as opposed to emotionally disconnected.

I feel safe (most times) being vulnerable because I created healthy boundaries, including around my empathy, and have consciously woven a network of friends, family, and my beloved who support me, almost unconditionally. It's so much less risky to put yourself out there, or to sit in discomfort, when you know you are deeply loved.

I'd love to hear from you all about experiences when you felt vulnerable, how you dealt with them, if they were negative or positive, and whether these were turning points in your lives. Tell us how you feel about vulnerability, if you've thought about it before, and if you've avoided it or embraced it.

### Salon Questionnaire

> What scenarios make you feel vulnerable?
> How do you behave when you feel vulnerable?
> How do you cope with, and even push through, those moments (and it's okay to say, "I don't")?
> Who supports you when you're being brave?
> Who tends to question you and hold you back? This can include yourself.
> Think of a time when you were really brave despite feeling vulnerable. How did you do that? How did you feel afterward?

### Breakouts: Questions for Discussion

> Is there a family member or well-known public figure you've noticed lean into and work through vulnerability in a way you admire?
> What's the bravest thing you've ever done? How did you feel at the time? Now?
> Have you ever done acting, public speaking, improv, or other

forms of performance in front of an audience? If so, was it something you chose to do or had to do because of your parents, school, or work? If not, what's holding you back?

## Large Group Questions

> Discuss the questions from the questionnaire round-robin style, and look for patterns among the group and individually.

## Closing

After considering the many ways the word *vulnerability* can be interpreted and expressed, how do you feel about it now? Reflect on a time when you were really brave, and thank your younger self for their strength to see a challenging situation through. Do this out loud, so you can really hear it and feel it. If there were wing-people involved, thank them, too. Vulnerability feels so much less risky when we know we are loved and supported.

## Quotes Selected by Salon Members

"At the moment, your resources for dealing with pain are unequal to your pain. The challenge, for the rest of your life, will be to change that." —Debra Spark, *Unknown Caller*

"Sorrow comes in great waves . . . but it rolls over us, and though it may almost smother us, it leaves us on the spot and we know that if it is strong, we are stronger, inasmuch as it passes and we remain." —Henry James

"The answers to the really big questions, the answers I most hunger for, don't ever come to us from the outside; rather, they come from a quiet place within. A place we can reach only when we find within ourselves the courage to pause, to abide for a while in that place of not knowing, to be at peace even with our uncertainties, and then to listen and attend with the ear of our own hearts."
—Katrina Kenison, *The Gift of an Ordinary Day*

"Uncertainty is where things happen. It is where the opportunities—for success, for happiness, for really living—are waiting." —Oliver Burkeman

"'The only people who see the whole picture,' he murmured, 'are the ones who step out of the frame.'" —Salman Rushdie, *The Ground Beneath Her Feet*

"We simply can't learn to be more vulnerable and courageous on our own. Sometimes our first and greatest dare is asking for support." —Brené Brown

## Finding and Nourishing Sanctuary Within and Without

One of my elderly neighbors brought to mind the concept of sanctuary when describing our neighborhood. We live in a suburban development built in the early 1960s, just a few miles from downtown Asheville, and within the city limits. We're bounded by the Blue Ridge Parkway, a strip of woods, and a four-lane that's not too bustling, but serves as the main route to our region's Veterans Affairs Medical Center. It's quiet here, most of the neighborhood roads end in cul-de-sacs. We share space with bears, foxes, bobcats, raccoons, coyotes, rabbits, groundhogs, and many birds, including red-tailed hawks and owls. Our brick ranchers are modest, the yards mostly lawns, though ambitious gardeners are springing up here and there creating "certified pollinator habitats," cottage-style gardens, and other kinds of floral beauty. The neighborhood is multi-generational and increasingly ethnically diverse.

My neighbor is one of a group I call the "original settlers," a resident since the time the homes were first built. She has spent the majority of her life here because it's safe and peaceful, and we look out for each other. During the pandemic, neighbors brought seating out to their lawns to greet passersby and hosted socially distanced gatherings. Some families set up card tables and ate their dinners and played games outside. Many put positive messaging on their front doors (I put a big handmade heart on ours) to reinforce the notion that we are a community, hoping to ease any worries that children or anxious folk might have had during such a strange and difficult time. It's not a perfect place (what is?), but for my elderly neighbor, and certainly for me, it's where we are at ease and can relax. If we need help, folks will do what they can. I've thought a lot about this idea of sanctuary my whole life, and I knew it would be a good one to explore now, when so many feel unsafe and disconnected from their neighbors.

"Finding and Nourishing Sanctuary" was a timely topic for us, especially in 2019, when salon members were feeling increasingly worn down by a divisive national political environment. Our salon offered a place to learn how we each created or sought out spaces that brought feelings of safety and nourishment. We shared tips on self-care and advice on making time for ourselves. It was a much-needed turn inward, to make sure that we carried the lamp for ourselves, as we did for others.

### Salon Description
Where are our sanctuaries? In places of worship, in the woods, by the sea, at home in a comfy chair with a cup of coffee, in a warm, fragrant bath, at yoga class, in the company of beloveds? What do we need to still our minds, calm our spirits, find ease, feel safe? In this salon we'll share our thoughts on sanctuaries and how each of us finds or creates these sacred spaces in our physical, emotional, and spiritual worlds.

### Prep Email
As we move toward our salon on sanctuary, let's think about our physical sanctuaries—those places we go to when we need to still our minds, calm our spirits, find ease, feel safe. Is there a room or part of a room in your house that is your sanctuary? What is it about the space (privacy or openness, sunny or dark, feng-shui position in the home, etc.), and what have you done to the space (painted a favorite color, created an altar, placed candles or flowers, set boundaries with other family members), that makes it a sanctuary for you? Is there an outside place that

offers sanctuary for you? What is it about this outside place that brings calm, ease, and a feeling of being safe?

## Teaser & Enricher
Try this exercise for one week: Place a picture of your favorite sanctuary by your bedside, work desk, or bathroom mirror, and put your phone in silent mode during your nonwork hours. Check in with yourself at the end of the week. How do you feel?

## Personal Backstory Shared at Salon
The word *sanctuary* has religious roots, and is defined as a sacred and consecrated place, as well as a place of refuge and protection. A place where you don't fear for your physical or emotional safety.

Churches have long served as temporary sanctuaries for those being sought by the law. They've also provided a refuge, at least fictionally, from vampires and other paranormal beings like trickster fairies and goblins. In this fantastic realm, holy water and crucifixes offer protection, extending a personal sanctuary zone around your body. When I was a child, and a fan of vampire movies, I would wear a crucifix to bed as protection, lying on my back, face up, so my crucifix would be visible on my chest to vampire intruders. It obviously worked, as I'm still here (and human)!

Sanctuary can be a physical space. It can also be a mental space. If you find yourself in a physical space that is unsafe and you are unable to leave, you can create a mental refuge to preserve your psyche.

My home is my sanctuary, my nest where I relax, recharge, create, am strong and unguarded. In earlier times of my life, my home did not feel safe for me physically or emotionally. I sought sanctuary elsewhere—in a yoga studio, in a Catholic lady chapel dedicated to Mary, by the sea, and in the woods. When I lived alone and felt unsafe, a friend performed a house blessing. She and a few friends moved from room to room as she ritually cleansed the space of negative energy and invited healing energy in. She completed the ceremony by calling upon four angels to sit at each corner of the roof and offer protection. The house blessing shifted things for me, and my house became my home, and my sanctuary.

When I'm stressed, when my eyes start to twitch, the usual sign of sensory overload, I find sanctuary in my bathtub, soaking for a good half hour before bed. I find similar ease in massage and healing touch, low lighting, candles, a clean space, soft fabrics, quiet or soothing music, nature sounds, or silence. I also find sanctuary in the company of friends and family, and sometimes in a city park, if people-watching doesn't involve distressing things. I find sanctuary in books, watching movies or TV, being intimate with my beloved, writing and creating art, working in the garden, and through hard, physical work. When I need to form a refuge in my head, I practice mindful breathing and visualizations.

## Salon Questionnaire

> Sanctuary is defined as a place of refuge and protection. A place where you don't fear for your physical or emotional safety. When you think of "sanctuary," what words come to mind?

> Where do you feel most triggered, most unsafe? How do you cope with this?

> What places are your sanctuaries? What is it about these places that offer you a way to find ease, to feel safe and calm?

> Which senses do you engage or disengage to create a physical sanctuary? Sound or silence, smell or no smell, taste or fasting, light or darkness, touch or isolation?

## Breakouts: Questions for Discussion

> How do you create a sanctuary in your mind? Meditation, yoga, vigorous exercise, mindful breathing, winding-down rituals, ingesting certain substances, using an app?

> Is your home a sanctuary? Why, or why not? Have you ever done a house blessing?

## Large Group Questions

> ➤ What is your favorite place that's a sanctuary, where you can feel safe, be calmed, let down your guard, and relax?
> ➤ Describe this place, and any role you had in creating or finding it.
> ➤ Do you prefer to be alone or in company in sanctuaries? Why?
> ➤ Let's have a round-robin discussion on how we create sanctuaries in our minds, offering our favorite methods—e.g., a ritual of some kind, a great app, a visualization, a soothing tea or other substance.

## Closing

I hope this salon is a sanctuary for you, that you feel safe to explore issues, and are comforted by the presence of other seekers with good hearts. By sharing about our sanctuaries, we learn new tools for ourselves, and also reflect on our triggers and how we cope with them. The world is very unsettling right now, and it is far too easy to get drawn into drama that we cannot solve, news that we cannot change. The practice of finding sanctuary within and without is vital to our physical and mental health. We need to let down our guards so that our nervous systems are not so taxed, so we can be happier and more peaceful humans. Onward on our healthy paths!

## Quotes Selected by Salon Members

"Each of us has an inner room where we can visit to be cleansed of fear-based thoughts and feelings. This room, the holy of holies, is a sanctuary of light."
—Marianne Williamson

"And into the forest I go, to lose my mind and find my soul." —John Muir

"Remember, the entrance to the sanctuary is inside you." —Rumi

"I am my own sanctuary and I can be reborn as many times as I choose throughout my life." —Lady Gaga

"Music was my refuge. I could crawl into the space between the notes and curl my back to loneliness." —Maya Angelou

"My dreams were all my own; I accounted for them to nobody; they were my refuge when annoyed—my dearest pleasure when free." —Mary Shelley

## WHERE ARE YOU IN #METOO?

This salon arose in response to the #MeToo movement when it was widely in the news. I wanted to talk about this movement in a women-only safe space. We, and by this I mean all the salon members, were undoubtedly thinking about the topic, and I guessed correctly that we'd have a lot to say about it. What I didn't anticipate, and should have, was how highly charged this salon would be. It was also interesting to hear one member, who is Cuban American, wonder what the movement would ultimately accomplish for BIPOC women, if it would change anything for those in more societally marginalized situations. She shared, "I think we tend to look at some of these movements through privileged lenses. Large corporate workplaces are shamed into taking action, either for PR reasons or good intentions or both, and we think that that takes care of the problem, but this has no bearing on the people who are most vulnerable."

In my recent interviews with salon members, several expressed appreciation that we explored #MeToo after we'd been meeting for a while because we'd built a safe container in our group and trusted each other. When planning your salon themes, it's always good to keep in mind where your group is around tough subjects—do you respect and trust each other well enough to talk about something so sensitive? Also consider how topics can build off each other, and thread together, in ways that serve the goals of your salon.

## Salon Description

#MeToo, an international movement against sexual harassment and assault, has inspired so many to come forward and name those who assaulted them. It has initiated purges of offenders from their jobs and prompted new codes of conduct at workplaces and conferences. How has #MeToo affected you? Did it spark painful memories from your past? Did you march in protests? Did it inspire you to get out the vote? Have you listened to other people share their stories? Do you think #MeToo is going too far? Let's discuss.

## Prep Email

In preparation for this salon, think about the ways the #MeToo movement has affected you. Have you experienced sexual harassment and assault? Have you witnessed it at school or at your workplace? Did you report it, or silently deal with it, even internalize it? Have you made any changes in your life— become more engaged, or retreated—because of it? What do you make of this movement and your part in it?

## Teaser & Enricher

Sometimes a subject is too hard to stare down or engage with alone. If this is true for you on this subject, consider reaching out to a friend or your therapist to discuss this topic before coming to this salon. Consider also taking a break from the news.

## Personal Backstory Shared at Salon

#MeToo has been such a big movement, international in scope and causing rapid change and rapid pushback. It's a perfect topic for us to discuss in our salon. Who among us has not been sexually harassed or assaulted? If you haven't, you surely know someone who has.

I was speaking with a woman author about a male author whom I met when our bookstore hosted him for an event. He came on to me at the dinner afterward (he told me he had an open marriage) and made sexual overtures that I quickly rebuffed. He wasn't an ogre, he didn't push himself on me, but it was odd, unwanted, and inappropriate. The woman author, about my age, knew this man well and shared how, at another event, he'd groped a woman while posing for a picture. She said that he was too old to change, and felt younger women were being too, in her words, "hard ass" on him and other men, like the *Paris Review* editor who resigned in 2017 after sexual misconduct. I responded that I was glad younger women didn't accept that kind of behavior anymore. I think we "older" women are so conditioned to accept bad behavior that we can take a beat or two longer to push back, or we may accept more than we should because we've been conditioned not to make waves. My hope is that as we evolve, and I pray this is rapidly, younger women will never tolerate this, and younger men won't even think of trying it. At a previous job, I was repeatedly sexually harassed by a female coworker and reported it to my female boss, who did nothing until I threatened legal action. Women need to evolve, too. We all do.

Because this is such a sensitive topic, let's all reaffirm that what people reveal here is confidential, so that we all feel safe when disclosing personal experiences.

### Salon Questionnaire
➢ Have you ever been sexually harassed or assaulted? How did you respond?
➢ Have you ever reported harassment at your workplace? How was this received?
➢ Has the #MeToo movement inspired you to speak up about something you'd kept quiet about?
➢ If so, did you 1) confront the abuser, or 2) make the event known to others in private conversations, via social media, to your employer, etc.?

### Breakouts: Questions for Discussion
➢ Have you made any changes in your life since #MeToo? If so, what changes?
➢ Do you feel #MeToo has gone too far? If yes, why or how?

> Do you feel #MeToo has made women safer? Why or why not?

## Large Group Questions
> What is your reaction to the #MeToo movement? Have you participated in this hashtag campaign?
> Has it impacted your understanding of or attitude toward sexual harassment and assault? If so, how? If not, why not?
> Do you think that talking about these issues can spur change? Why or why not?

## Closing
Where are you in #MeToo now, after this salon? Do you think this is a watershed moment in our culture, a turning point in the ways people talk about and react to sexual misconduct? Or do you think things will simply return, or have already returned, to the way they've always been? Wherever we might go from here, we can draw comfort from knowing we have each other as witnesses and support in our healing and individual journeys. We are not alone.

## Quotes Selected by Salon Members
"When you experience trauma and meet other people that have a similar experience, and you show empathy for each other, it creates a bond." —Tarana Burke, founder of the #MeToo movement

"I was taught the way of progress was neither swift nor easy." —Marie Curie

"It's not about perfection. It's about purpose. We have to care about our bodies and what we put in them. Women have to take the time to focus on our mental health—take time for self, for the spiritual, without feeling guilty or selfish. The world will see you the way you see you, and treat you the way you treat yourself." —Beyoncé

"If we tell the truth to each other, we empower each other. It helps us understand that there's no such thing as perfect. There's unique, but not perfect." —Gloria Steinem

"Continue to embrace the things that make you unique even if it makes others uncomfortable. You are enough. And whenever you feel in doubt, whenever you want to give up, you must always remember to choose freedom over fear." —Janelle Monáe

"One molecule makes a ripple that creates a wave that changes the shoreline." —Paula M. Reeves

## THE THINGS THAT MATTER

This salon grew out of a conversation with a friend, and a growing realization that I was not making enough time for activities that feed me personally. I'm a doer and an organizer, and I was always prioritizing utilitarian life admin tasks over walks in the woods, live music, hanging with friends, writing, or playing my flute. There's no question I'll always get those life admin tasks done as I'm hyper-responsible. But I was sacrificing cherished parts of my life to the god of productivity. After working on scheduling me-time, however I wanted to spend it, I now experience more happiness and energy and variety in my daily life. Interestingly, pre-Covid era, inspired by the "Things That Matter" salon, my husband and I decided to approach our city like tourists. We made a plan to check out the venues and vistas that attract people all over the world to Asheville. We would visit every rooftop bar and enjoy the views. We also wanted to take in more live music, especially by those musicians whose music had been part of our lives since childhood, shaping who we are. Over a summer, we met our goals on all fronts, enjoying gorgeous sunsets while sipping delicious cocktails, and seeing some classic music acts. We had a blast. During the Covid era, when the bars and concert halls were closed, I treasured those memories all the more. If that time taught us anything, and hopefully it has taught us much, you never know what can happen, so seize the day! Make time in your life for the things that matter; you won't regret it.

You also won't regret choosing this as a salon topic. Talking about how you prioritize (or don't) what feeds you spiritually and emotionally will lead to a dynamic and deeply personal conversation. As members of our salon shared which parts of their lives they most cherish and what goals they hoped to achieve, we crowdsourced our best tips on how to honor and make time for what really mattered to them. I came away from our salon scheduling personal time in my Google calendar on repeat. I didn't want to check back a year later and discover I hadn't made time for the things that matter. Do you?

## Salon Description
"Things that matter" are the ways we express ourselves, learn and evolve, engage with community, exercise, and love. These are the experiences that make our hearts sing, nourish us, and give us the strength to go on during hard stretches. Are we making time for them? Let's discuss!

## Prep Email
To prep for this salon, come up with a list of three things that really matter to you. These can be anything, from planting a flower garden or getting your book proposal out to agents, to tending to relationships by setting up coffee dates with friends and reaching out to family. List them and think about where you are in relation to them, and if anything is getting in the way of spending more time on them.

## Teaser & Enricher
If you had to choose just one activity that matters to your heart or a life goal, what would it be? Can you schedule one hour of doing that activity this week?

## Personal Backstory Shared at Salon

Clara is my bullet journal mentor, and someone I look to when it comes to organizing my life. She's smart and creative, infusing beauty and elegance into whatever she takes on. She's also extremely responsible about getting life admin stuff done. We're so similar in ways like this that we joke we're sisters from another mother. When meeting her in a café near her home for coffee, she shared that she'd noticed she was making time for all those life admin tasks that kept her life running smoothly, but she wasn't making time for "the things that mattered," those activities that fed her emotionally and brought her joy and satisfaction. She recalled describing to a friend a day filled with "things that matter" as one in which she didn't do much because she was not particularly "productive." Yet, she realized that those "things that mattered" were the ones most meaningful to the health of her mind and spirit. Deciding to rectify this, she made a list of six things that mattered to her, and put them into her scheduler, the way she would put work and life admin tasks, to make sure they were prioritized and happened consistently. She knows she's the type of person who will *always* get the life admin stuff done, so no need to worry about deprioritizing them. What she needed to do was prioritize and center those things that were personally important. She also had to work on her narrative to support the things that matter and not diminish their importance.

I loved this! It's so easy to skip scheduling time to move forward projects and experiences that are close to our hearts. I looked at my bullet journal, which also serves as my planner, anew. I thought about the things that mattered and scheduled them during the times of day and days of the week when my brain and body would most likely achieve them. Writing in the morning and on Fridays, creative play after work, Pilates every Tuesday afternoon, and so on. I also put these activities in my Google calendar, on repeat. Since I began this, I've made real progress in many areas. Life goes by quickly. Don't put yourself, and your heart's desire, last.

## Salon Questionnaire

> What matters to you? "Things that matter" are the things, which could include specific people or objects, that bring joy and fulfillment, that make you deeply happy. Identify up to six things that matter this way to you.

> Are you making time for the things that matter? Okay, now flip open your planner or look at the calendar on your phone. Think about what you did last week, last month. Did you make time for any of the things you just listed? Do you see them in your schedule? Briefly describe your success or challenge(s) in making time for the things that matter.

> Here are some tactics to make time for things that matter: Listen to your body, limit distractions (including social media and life admin), group your life admin tasks for one day or time of day each week, schedule things that matter consistently. Can you do at least one of these things this week? Do you need an accountability buddy to make it happen? Who will cheer you on?

## Breakouts: Questions for Discussion

> What gets in the way of making time for things that matter? (This could be you.)

> What are some ways you could address this?

> Do you have an accountability buddy who supports your efforts?

## Large Group Questions

> Please share the top two or three things that matter on your list. Why did you put them there?

> What is the most common thing that gets in the way of doing things for yourself? (This could be you.)

> Language counts. The words we use to describe accomplishing things that matter, life admin, and everything in between are important because as we think them, say them aloud, and write about them, they form a narrative we internalize and believe. Think about how you refer to activities you cherish. Do you recognize, even for the listener, their importance? Do you give these activities a place of honor?

## Closing

Make a vow to yourself. Starting today, make a vow to put the things that matter front and center in your life. Enlist buddies, your family, your planner and calendar, to open the space and honor what makes you deeply happy, what makes you fulfilled. A long and healthy life isn't a guarantee. Let's fill what time we do have with as much joy and love and meaning as we can. And if you need help, we're all there for you.

## Quotes Selected by Salon Members

"Everyone has been made for some particular work, and the desire for that work has been put in every heart. Let yourself be silently drawn by the stronger pull of what you really love." —Rumi

"The universe buries strange jewels deep within us all, and then stands back to see if we can find them." —Elizabeth Gilbert, *Big Magic*

"When you recover or discover something that nourishes your soul and brings joy, care enough about yourself to make room for it in your life." —Jean Shinoda Bolen

"If you have dreams you want to pursue, the time is now. There is no perfect time, and there is no better time. There is only the time you lose while you're making excuses." —Holly Lisle

"What if you wake up some day, and you're 65, or 75, and you never got your memoir or novel written; or you didn't go swimming in warm pools and oceans all those years because your thighs were jiggly and you had a nice big comfortable tummy; or you were just so strung out on perfectionism and people-pleasing that you forgot to have a big juicy creative life, of imagination and radical silliness and staring off into space like

when you were a kid? It's going to break your heart."
—Anne Lamott

"You're worried about how you're going to feel at the
end of your life? What about right now? Live. Right this
minute. That's where the joy's at." —Abigail Thomas

"Begin doing what you want to do now. We are not
living in eternity. We have only this moment, sparkling
like a star in our hand—and melting like a snowflake."
—Francis Bacon

## LET'S TALK ABOUT ANGER

In a palette of emotions, anger is enigmatic, at least for me. I tend
to access that emotion less than others, but it's there, of course. A
friend once told me that when she was angry, she liked to smash
eggs. My first thought: What a waste of eggs! I don't know if it's
my frugality, or some kind of disconnect, but breaking things in
anger, or to release anger, is just not in my nature. Better to hit a
thousand tennis balls against a wall, exhaust myself in garden-
ing, or soak it off in a long bath. But I get it. I can step over the
line from impatience to anger when I feel my needs are disre-
spected, when my voice in an important conversation is ignored
or shut down. I get angry over injustice and cruelty to me and to
others. Anger prods me into action, to wake up to a situation.
But I've found that in these instances a pause and a plan help me
act more wisely and effectively, though that isn't always how it
plays out. Anger is real and if we don't deal with it, it takes up
residence in our bodies in unhealthy ways.

Because women are often criticized for expressing anger or
described as being exaggeratedly fearful when it is expressed in
their presence, I thought it would be a perfect subject to talk
about salon-style. It was! We brought our unique family and
cultural experiences with anger into the conversation, and had
much to say about how we felt expressing this emotion and
being in its presence. This topic could be triggering for some,
especially for victims of domestic violence, so I recommend

being aware of what might come up when communicating with salon members about it.

## Salon Description

We're living in a time when women (cis and trans) and nonbinary people are expressing their anger in brave and powerful ways. For many, expressing anger is energizing. For others, it is exhausting, and not an emotion that they are comfortable feeling or receiving. How do you experience anger? How does it feel when someone expresses their anger toward you? Let's talk about it!

## Prep Email

As we head into a salon on anger, think about what this emotion means to you and the frequency with which it arises in your life, either from within, or in your presence, including being directed at you. Is anger an emotion that you're comfortable feeling, expressing, and being around, an emotion like any other, or is it an emotion that makes you particularly uncomfortable, even fearful?

## Teaser & Enricher

If you use a mindfulness app like Calm or Headspace or Healthy Minds Program, consider upgrading to a family plan to bring in some family or friends for the next year. Meditation and breath awareness are helpful ways to counter the effects of repressed or unprocessed anger in the body.

## Personal Backstory Shared at Salon

I wrote a piece on anger for my sister blog, *Barrett Sisters*. Thinking about this emotion really opened my eyes to how I process it, hold it in my body, and deal with being in the presence of an angry person. I once saw a man work metal over a fire. He said to watch the color of the metal as it sat in the flames, changing from black to red to orange to yellow, then white. White is the hottest, when metal becomes soft for shaping. While I observed him work, my thoughts went to anger and its many shades, from annoyance, to displeasure, to hostility, to rage. My anger usually arises as a slow burn or a brief stabbing pain, rarely flaring to anything more. Instead of building to the point of rage, I cry, feeling profound disappointment that things have come to such a pass. The impulse to throw and break things, or to strike another person—I've never felt that. I'm slow to anger and quick to rid myself of it. After releasing anger, I don't feel better; I'm exhausted, and remorseful if I've hurt someone in the process.

This is not to say I don't get angry. I can work up a righteous anger to protect someone I love, or any vulnerable person or creature, if they are harmed. I get angry when I see children or animals neglected or otherwise ill-treated, when someone is unfairly spoken about, when there is injustice. I have a strong guardian nature. I know anger has its place, and I honor that. Anger can spark change. It certainly has for me. Let's talk about the place of anger in our lives.

## Salon Questionnaire

> If you were to make a pie chart of your emotions, how big would the anger slice be?
> What activities or personality types trigger your anger, including anger at yourself? Describe a few of them.
> How do you feel anger in your body? Do you get physical, raise your voice, tremble, cry, feel powerful, get hot, laugh, etc.?
> When you realize you're angry, how do you process it? For example, take direct action, do some introspection, journal, call friends or family, eat or drink too much, binge-watch TV, etc.?

## Breakouts: Questions for Discussion

> How was anger expressed in your family home?
> Did the women and girls express it differently than the men and boys?
> Do you remember something in your childhood that made you really angry?

> Did your anger help resolve this situation?

**Large Group Questions**
> Can you remember the last time you were really angry? Why? What did you do about it?
> How do you feel anger in your body? Do you get physical, raise your voice, tremble, cry, feel powerful, get hot, laugh, etc.
> Would you describe yourself as hot-tempered?
> How do you respond when you have to engage with an angry person?

**Closing**
A salon member shared with me, "As someone who is generally very bubbly, I often feel embarrassed when I become angry, even if the anger is justified. And as someone who spent her early career in a traditionally male-dominated workplace, I've been called a shrew more than once for simply speaking at the same volume as the males in the room." After this discussion tonight, consider if your attitude toward anger has shifted, if you are more accepting of, even supportive of, feeling it, expressing it, and respecting its place in our emotional palettes. If you're still feeling uneasy about anger, it might be well worth exploring further.

**Quotes Selected by Salon Members**
"Telling me to relax or smile when I'm angry is like bringing a birthday cake into an ape sanctuary. You're just asking to get your genitals bitten off." —Amy Poehler

"Anger has been a tremendously healing tool for me. My rage is really keeping me alive, my rage is my art. We're always told by therapists and clergy and mentors that you need to forgive and heal, and I'm not there, and I don't plan on going there." —Margaret Cho

"At many events where I am speaking about feminism,

young women ask how they can comport themselves so they aren't perceived as angry while they practice their feminism. They ask this question as if anger is an unreasonable emotion when considering the inequalities, challenges, violence, and oppression women the world over face. I want to tell these young women to embrace their anger, sharpen themselves against it." —Roxane Gay

"I refuse to accept that there's a sort of duality between fact and emotion. If we were to lose the ability to be emotional, if we were to lose the ability to be angry, to be outraged, we would be robots. And I refuse that. And partly, the reason that they say the arguments are emotional is because they don't want to face the facts." —Arundhati Roy

"You should be angry. You must not be bitter. Bitterness is like cancer. It eats upon the host. It doesn't do anything to the object of its displeasure. So use that anger. You write it. You paint it. You dance it. You march it. You vote it. You do everything about it. You talk it. Never stop talking it." —Maya Angelou

"A good therapist once told me that you should get angry as many times a day as you visit the bathroom. I think what she meant was, first, that anger is natural. You may not like it, but it has its place and, depending on your temperament, it may be a constant in your life. She also meant that anger arrives on its own schedule and for its own purposes, and its schedule may be different from yours." —Thomas Moore

## STRONG WOMEN: LOOKING INWARD, LOOKING OUT

I was once told that when I presented strongly, especially around my anger, I expressed it in a masculine way. My "presentation" was aggressive and provocative, and if a man struck out at me in response, either verbally or physically, I had it coming. When

I was younger and confused about a lot of things, including my sense of self and worth, I accepted this assessment as truth. I tried to be "softer," or whatever being female while feeling strong emotions was supposed to be. I now recognize this all to be deeply misogynistic, a way of shutting me down. Sadly, it's not uncommon for women who present strongly, whether at work, in social situations, or personally, to be bashed by men, and even other women, as masculine, freakish, ugly, and deserving of whatever they get, especially if it's bad.

A conversation with other women about what it means to be strong and female was a great way to explore our feelings about the topic, and society's feelings, too. We engaged in some collective soul-searching around the degree to which we've internalized negative responses to strong women, as opposed to strong men. We considered how we express ourselves and whether we diminished our authority in our word and wardrobe choices. We didn't want to have to emulate men to be seen as strong, but we also grappled with what strength can look like in women, and how we could support that in others and in ourselves.

This salon could be adapted for a mixed gender group. Strength, especially when manifested for the first time or infrequently in certain settings, can challenge existing power balances between individuals, in families, among friends, and in workplaces. Sometimes that challenge is welcome, but at other times it can feel threatening. Although we are centering women in this starter kit, I invite you to amend to fit the needs and identities of your group.

### Salon Description

How do you react to a strong, confident woman? What if she's your boss, your political candidate, a woman who works for a candidate or organization you despise, your mother or sister, your best friend? Is her gender something you factor, perhaps unconsciously, into your reaction? Are you a harsher critic of strong women than strong men?

How do we view ourselves? When you present strongly to family, at work, or in public, how has it been received? Do you choose to appear less strong in order to please and not intimidate? Upon reflection, do you undermine yourself in your physical presentation (hair, dress, makeup), speech patterns, or aversion to risk-taking?

How can we be our strongest? Think about ways you impair your leadership and confidence, and ways you support those qualities. Not everyone wants to lead others, but we do lead our own lives, and we are stewards of our experience. Let's see how we can help each other be, as one strong woman put it, "stronger together." We are all strong women; let's share our secrets and our struggles.

### Prep Email
Taking physical strength out of your considerations, when you think of a woman as strong, what qualities come to mind? Do you share any of those qualities? Would you describe yourself as a strong person? Why or why not? What feelings come up?

### Teaser & Enricher
Please bring one item that represents a triumph. This will be part of an Altar of Womanly Triumphs that will inspire us during the salon.

### Personal Backstory Shared at Salon
I chose the theme of strong women as it's been on my mind a lot. In 2016, we watched a woman presidential candidate be relentlessly attacked regarding her appearance—her hair, her pantsuits, her voice, the list goes on. I noticed this same thing happening to a woman who worked closely with the rival candidate, watched as the media and my friends on Facebook were being cruel about her appearance. My husband, Jon, and I were talking in a snarky way about her when I suddenly heard ourselves and said to Jon, "We need to stop. We're being sexist." He agreed. We stopped. Making fun of their appearance is one of the most common ways people silence women. I was reminded of a Facebook post by Elizabeth Gilbert, "Dear Women, Be Kind to Other Women," in which she writes, "My

experience is this: once we have decided where we land on that scale of beauty, we tend to judge all the other women who have made different decisions in either direction around us: This woman is too vain; that one is too plain . . . it never ends. It also bothers me that women who define themselves as liberal, left-wing feminists (like myself) will stand on a picket line to defend the right of another woman to do whatever she wants with her reproductive system—but then attack that woman for what she decided to do to her face. Let me break it down for you: It's none of your business."

I was again mulling over the subject of strong women during my honeymoon when I was reading Tara Mohr's *Playing Big: Practical Wisdom for Women Who Want to Speak Up, Create, and Lead.* Mohr describes how we undermine our own female power because of insecurity, often caused by how we are raised and our culture's generally harsh attitude toward powerful, strong women. We might adopt a soft voice, use verbal hedges and tics like "I'm not an expert . . .," "I could be wrong, but . . .," or "Does that make sense?" or we don't speak at all—we stay silent. We wait forever to take a decisive step because we fear making a mistake. We diminish ourselves because we believe that calling attention to our value, worth, and contribution is unseemly.

We might now consider why we are doing these things, and if they aren't serving us, stop. I want to stop. I've been looking at my self-undermining habits and addressing them, though some of them are so a part of me now, it's difficult. A former boss and mentor, Wanda, encouraged me to "step into your majesty." I wrote her advice down on a Post-it and keep it taped to my computer monitor as a daily reminder to not diminish myself. For those of you who are seeking to restore or strengthen your power, I hope you find what you need from this salon.

## Salon Questionnaire

> ➢ What is a strong woman to you? List some adjectives you associate with strong women.
> ➢ How do you react to a strong, confident woman? List some

emotions that rise up.
> Write one sentence about when you felt strongest.
> Write one sentence about when you felt weakest.

## Breakouts: Questions for Discussion
> Do you have a real-life or fictional female strong woman role model?
> When you present strongly to family, at work, or in public, how has it been received?
> Do you choose to present less strongly in order to please and not intimidate? In what way(s)?
> Do you undermine yourself in your physical presentation (hair, dress, makeup), speech patterns, or aversion to risk-taking?

## Large Group Questions
> Share some of the words you use to describe strong women.
> Share the one sentence from the questionnaire describing when you felt strongest.
> Does anyone want to elaborate on their strong moment? Did you prepare for it? How did you feel after?
> Let's talk a few minutes about each object people brought with them for our Altar of Womanly Triumphs. Please get your object, if you'd like, and tell us why you chose it.

## Closing
Strength has many faces; the word means different things within our group. In all instances, though, being strong means honoring yourself and expressing yourself in a way that reflects who you are at your essence. That can mean being quiet or being loud. We support each other in being our strongest selves, in whatever ways that is manifest, because it is a brave thing in this world to be a strong woman.

## Quotes Selected by Salon Members
"If we maintain our radiance and enter a situation with radiance, often radiance will come our way." —Patti Smith

"You gain strength, courage, and confidence by every experience in which you really stop to look fear in the face. You are able to say to yourself, 'I have lived through this horror. I can take the next thing that comes along.' You must do the thing you think you cannot do." —Eleanor Roosevelt

"I am willing to put myself through anything; temporary pain or discomfort means nothing to me as long as I can see that the experience will take me to a new level." —Diana Nyad

"There is no greater agony like bearing an untold story inside of you." —Maya Angelou

"When you have done everything that you can do, surrender. Give yourself up to the power and energy that's greater than yours." —Oprah Winfrey

## THE SENSES: WHAT INSPIRES, SOOTHES, AND TURNS US ON

Noticing sensual things—the play of light across clouds at sunrise and sunset, the smell of air as we transition into a new season, the feel of clothing against my skin, the taste of coffee and cream on my tongue as I take my first sip in the morning, the sound of geese honking and flapping their wings as they come in for a landing at the ponds where I walk every day—is such a part of who I am. When I'm stressed, I ground and soothe by immersing myself more fully in my senses, with aromatherapy, a warm bath, candles, quiet music, soft pajamas, comfort food. When I set the scene for romance or a party, a similar dance around the house involves creating a sensual backdrop to influence mood, including my own. Do you ever notice when you're so cut off from your senses, living in your head and not in your body, that you bump into things, forget to eat, look and maybe smell like something that emerged from under a rock? Not good!

At this salon gathering, members included a baker, a composer, several artists, an interior designer, an architect, writers, a healthcare worker, a realtor, and an educator. Our livelihoods covered taste, sound, sight, touch, and smell. I was curious how members were influenced by the sensual world, how they tapped into it, and whether an affinity for certain senses may have influenced their choice of profession. If you find your group representing many of the senses, it would be interesting to note that as well and bring that into your discussion. I purposely hosted this salon at the start of the winter holiday season because it's a time of so much stimulation that we need reminders to slow down and take care of ourselves and savor life.

## Salon Description
Does a certain sound, smell, taste, color, or tactile sensation transport you to another time in your life? A whiff of Love's Baby Soft perfume sends me right back to my early teen years, as does every time I hear Boston's "More Than a Feeling." Without ever eating it again (and I have no plans to), I can viscerally recall the taste of Howard Johnson's macaroni and cheese topped with ketchup, a staple in our childhood home. Do you time travel through your senses, too?

When you want to relax or get into a sexy mood, do you soothe or awaken your senses? Does your creative expression or career path involve one sense over the others? In this salon we'll discuss our relationship with our senses, and inspire each other to explore a less-noticed or less-engaged sense, to enrich our lives.

## Prep Email
In preparation for our upcoming salon, consider: Do you have a dominant sense? If you had to lose one sense, what would it be?

## Teaser & Enricher
I've been thinking about my sensual interaction with the world as we head toward our salon and am enjoying this focus. Please bring something to the salon that reflects a significant sensual experience for you—a perfume, a painting or photograph, an audio sample, something edible, something that feels wonder-

ful. It can be one thing or several, whatever you're moved to bring. If you want to share something that has a negative effect on your senses, please give us a heads up as some of us may want to avoid it (I definitely don't want to smell mold!).

## Personal Backstory Shared at Salon

In just the first hour of our salon, during our potluck, we've engaged all our senses. We've experienced taste through eating, and taken in the scent of the food, each other, the aromatherapy diffuser. We've looked around this setting, and we've touched each other, our utensils, the food to our tongues, and more. We've listened to each other's voices and to the music in the background. Engaging the senses, tapping into the sensual world more deeply, is a way of slowing down, stopping to smell the roses . . . or the coffee or the subtle aroma of a glass of wine.

When I lived on a farm and was really stressed, I would go outside with my journal and colored pencils and draw whatever was around me. I would sit by a creek in front of my home and draw rocks, the plants springing up around them, and water, where it escaped from the creek and pooled in crevices among the rocks and clods of earth. I looked very deeply at these things, at their colors, textures, shapes, the way they touched each other. I also noted the movement of air bending a leaf or skittering a fragment of dirt across a stone, the heat of the sun on my skin, the crunch of gravel when a car passed by on the road above me, the sound of water rushing along the creek bed. It was very grounding and freed me from a cycle of rumination, bringing me into the present.

It's my hope that in the next hour we become inspired to engage more deeply in our dominant sense, and also awaken appreciation for the other senses, including that one we might give up if we had to (recall the discussion prompt from my email), or if life took it away through illness or aging.

Let's talk about the senses.

## Salon Questionnaire

> * On a scale of 1–5, with 5 being the highest, how engaged are you with your senses?
> * Is one of your senses particularly sensitive? Do you have a sensitivity to light, smell, taste, touch, sound?
> * Do you consider yourself someone who lives more in their head or their body?
> * Do you intensify or limit sensory stimulation when you need to relax? Why is that?

## Breakouts: Questions for Discussion

> * What is your dominant sense? Why do you think it is dominant?
> * What is your second most aware sense?
> * If you had to give up one sense, what would it be? Why? What would be lost?

## Large Group Question

> * I asked each of you to bring something that has personal sensual significance. Let's go around and everyone share what you brought, identifying the sense it connects with for you, and what you love or hate about this thing.

## Closing

As we enter a season that can cause our minds to be overloaded with so much clutter, it's a perfect time to reconnect and nourish our sensual selves, to be in our bodies, and experience the richness of our senses, the flipside of the commercial aspect of the coming weeks of this holiday season. Becoming more sensually aware is a perfect way to slow down and really be in the moment; we can more quickly appreciate the richness of the world we're in, and also notice those things that aren't pleasing to us and escape or remove them, if possible.

## Quotes Selected by Salon Members

"At the doorway of the senses, the self chances upon the world." —Diane Ackerman

"Touch comes before sight, before speech. It is the first language and the last, and it always tells the truth."
—Margaret Atwood

"Smell is a potent wizard that transports you across thousands of miles and all the years you have lived."
—Helen Keller

"Children, like animals, use all their senses to discover the world. Then artists come along and discover it the same way, all over again." —Eudora Welty

"For the sense of smell, almost more than any other, has the power to recall memories and it is a pity that we use it so little." —Rachel Carson

## AGING AND ITS DISCONTENTS (AND PLEASANT SURPRISES)

This is a great topic for a multigenerational group to explore together. For my group of women over fifty, it was timely and topical. We've crossed a Rubicon; we can no longer pretend, even to ourselves, that we're "young." In a sense, this can be freeing, to embrace who we are, how we look now, and, when possible, embody the power and authority that can come with being the oldest person in the room.

For a younger salon group, discussing aging can be eye-opening. When people are getting Botox and fillers in their teens and twenties, when the percentage of women coloring their hair to cover up grey has grown from 7 percent in 1950 to over 80 percent today, it's clear that physical signs of aging are something that, in our culture, we seek to hide more than ever. It's like we're trying to stay in a holding pattern of forever-forty (or thirty, or twenty) for the rest of our lives. How exhausting!

Another challenge we all can experience, regardless of gender or age, is feeling increasingly invisible to the sensual gaze of others. We are diminished at the same time we are becoming more discerning and sensually aware.

As a heads-up to hosts: There are strong feelings out there about what we do to our bodies around aging, and how well or poorly we've set ourselves up financially for retirement. Aging might not be the most popular topic you discuss, but it's one of the most important. We shy away from discussing aging the way we avoid talking about death, though both are inevitable, unless we're struck down in our youth. I believe that the more elders share how they've successfully negotiated this stage of life, and the more younger people open up about their thoughts and fears about aging, the more likely it is we can turn this anti-aging ship around and honor the process.

## Salon Description

With honesty and open hearts, let's explore our experiences with aging, and our hopes and fears for the future. My goal for us is a real (platitude-free) discussion of a subject that confronts us all.

## Prep Email

Some things to consider before we meet:

> Was there a moment when you realized you were leaving your "youth" and becoming "older"?
> Do you carry fear about aging? If so, what are your top three fears?
> What positives have come into your life as you age? Name three.
> Has your work/life balance changed?
> Has your sex life or view of yourself as sexual or sexy changed?
> Is there anything about your appearance that you've newly embraced? Enhanced?

## Teaser & Enricher

Is there a person older than you whom you admire? Consider putting their picture near your bathroom mirror or on a personal altar to inspire you as we move toward the salon. If they are still alive, write to them and share your admiration.

**Personal Backstory Shared at Salon**

My goal tonight is for us to leave with many seeds for private thoughts and future conversations. We will likely only be able to touch upon the first few layers of our feelings about aging because I want to balance our discussion between the challenges and blessings of aging. So, starting in: According to AARP's research on women who are fifty years and older, and echoed in research by the National Council on Aging, some of the top fears for women as they age are:

> Becoming less attractive, becoming "invisible"
> Being left alone
> Not having enough money to pay for all needs
> Cancer and other health concerns
> Being dependent on others
> Caring for others

Our culture does not treat aging very supportively. We evolve, but are still youth-obsessed. Even though there is much said about the influence of baby boomers on advertising, we still see so many products that scream "I'm hip, I'm young, I am NOT old!"

This quote by Lori Day in her article, "Aging While Female Is Not Your Worst Nightmare," epitomizes this: "I look like a typical 51-year-old, and it is just bizarre realizing that my appearance is something many young women dread. Ageism is a life-altering injustice affecting women in ways that are different than the effects on men." Ageism affects everyone, but women are hit hardest, often finding it much more difficult to get higher-level employment as they age, and, if heterosexual, to partner with a man their age. Why wouldn't our life experience result in increased value, rather than less, in both realms? We must work for change, and support others during this current wave of feminist activism, so that negative concepts around aging will fall away.

I remember a woman in my yoga class speaking up about how tired she was of hearing how great you'd feel when you took yoga. Despite practicing yoga regularly, her body hurt all the time. She was probably in her late fifties, which felt ancient to me then. Her comments prompted me to imagine what it felt like to be in an older body, to deal with arthritis and creaky, inflamed joints. My yoga teacher, who was a similar age to this student, shared that a consistent yoga practice would help us to build and maintain flexibility, strength, and balance. We might not feel "good" in our bodies the way we did when we were younger, but we'd be more likely to avoid injury or, down the road, the need to live in an assisted care facility. I began to notice that in our yoga class, and later, when I started Pilates, the elders who really knew their bodies were stronger and more disciplined than people my age. It just took reframing, and more information, to open my eyes to a completely new way of looking at aging.

I have concerns about my abilities to live with dignity in my old age, and be in community with others who have lively minds and are creative. I don't want to become paranoid or embittered, living alone behind shuttered windows, curtains drawn, the way a ninety-nine-year-old neighbor does, who refuses our help to bring in her garbage bins, and shuffles away in her housecoat and slippers. When I visited my mother's nursing home, she was a beacon among very aging minds. That's a hard place to be, though she had a positive attitude and a loving, compassionate heart. I've been very disciplined to live as debt-free as possible, funnel a good portion of my income into a retirement account, and pay off my mortgage by retirement age. I'm doing what I can.

## Salon Questionnaire

> Was there a moment when you realized you were getting "older"? How old were you when this happened?
> What are your three biggest fears about aging?
> How do you address these fears (it's okay to say, "I don't")?
> What does your future financial picture look like? Have you made plans for your retirement and eldercare? (Most women don't, so if you haven't, you're not alone.)
> What have you achieved since you've turned thirty, forty, fifty, etc. that you never would have thought possible when you were younger?

## Breakouts: Questions for Discussion
> ➤ What is the single best thing so far about your current age? What is the worst?
> ➤ How are you taking care of your body?
> ➤ Have you changed any self-care, eating, or drinking habits as you've aged?

## Large Group Discussion
> ➤ Let's talk about our fears around aging. Let's go around and each speak of one or two fears we have.
> ➤ What are one or two goals for this current season of your life?
> ➤ What positives have come into your life as you've aged? Are you more in control of decisions? Is your work/life balance better? Is sex better?
> ➤ Is there anything about your appearance that you've newly embraced? Enhanced?

## Closing
The Black Swan Salon represents people in three different decades of middle age. Our discussion on this topic offered windows and mirrors around aging and associated concerns. A group that is mixed gender, or has a wider age spread, would offer even more views into realities and concerns about aging for a variety of lived experiences. I suggest reflecting on the make-up of your group and acknowledging what may have come up in the discussion before asking, "What changes can you make now to create your best possible future? How can you address your fears? What can you let go?"

## Quotes Selected by Salon Members
"To live in this world you must be able to do three things: to love what is mortal; to hold it against your bones knowing your own life depends on it; and when the time comes to let it go, to let it go." —Mary Oliver

"Beautiful young people are accidents of nature, but beautiful old people are works of art." —Eleanor Roosevelt

"I think your whole life shows in your face and you should be proud of that." —Lauren Bacall

"Age has no reality except in the physical world. The essence of a human being is resistant to the passage of time. Our inner lives are eternal, which is to say that our spirits remain as youthful and vigorous as when we were in full bloom." —Gabriel García Márquez

"Old age ain't no place for sissies." —Bette Davis

## Birthing a Dream & Letting Something Go

This is the perfect salon to hold in January, or anytime significant to you and your group when you want to commit to following a dream. The inspiration for this salon comes from the Kansas Leadership Center, which led a wrap-up session for an American Booksellers Association's conference in 2016. As a way to integrate our experience of the conference, we wrote down specific goals for our bookstores, three steps we viewed as important to make them happen, what partners we could engage to help us move them forward, what challenges stood in the way, and how we'd measure success. Such a methodical approach can help birth the loftiest dream. What do we want, who can help us, what are the potential obstacles, and how do we define success?

My favorite weddings include an officiant who enlists the vows of those present to support the couple on their journey. We become their accountability partners. The couple is making a lifetime commitment to marriage, and we are there to help them when life throws obstacles in their way. They are not alone. I'm a big fan of accountability partners, or buddies, because they become our teammates, helping us move a dream forward toward the goals we've set for ourselves.

In my interviews with salon members, the special element for this salon—mailing a letter to our future selves to check on how we were doing with birthing our dreams—came up repeatedly. For one, the letter clarified that it was not the time to pursue the dream. She shared, "I knew then that it would take me becoming an empty nester before my goals around writing would really happen, but it was good to see that I still wanted those things, and would eventually make them happen." For another, receiving the letter was extremely affirming, as she'd made great progress with her plans, and appreciated her past self's encouraging words. It's always a surprise, akin to unexpected time travel, to find a letter in your mailbox with very familiar handwriting on the envelope, containing words written by an earlier version of you. Try it!

### Salon Description

Is there a dream—traveling to a place you've always wanted to visit, submitting your art or writing for publication, learning a new skill like cooking or dancing, becoming more financially secure, finding a partner or leaving one—that you would love to experience this year? How can you realize, or at least make progress toward achieving, this dream? What's been stopping you? In our salon we'll have the opportunity to share a dream, small or big, examine what might stop us, and consider what we need to put in place to birth it.

### Prep Email

Think about one thing—activity, object, relationship, or accomplishment—that has always called to you as a dream to pursue. When, a year from now, you look back, what progress in realizing this dream would feel meaningful?

### Teaser & Enricher

Provide paper and envelopes at the salon and ask members, as a final exercise before the close, to write one thing they'd like to accomplish in the coming year, what challenges they need to overcome to make it happen, and how they'd measure success. They will address the envelopes to themselves and insert their notes. At some time in the future (three to six months) mail them their letters as a way to check in on progress.

**Personal Backstory Shared at Salon**
I wanted to touch back on why I created this salon, and also why it has its name, Black Swan Salon. Black swans can symbolize deep mysteries within us that are longing to be set free to express themselves creatively. My desire with this group is to explore and express these mysteries, and see where this leads us, which in my mind can only be in a positive direction. In *The Power of Eight,* author Lynne McTaggart discusses the proven potential of working in small groups to heal our lives. By working with group intention and consciousness, what we send out comes back to us magnified. That is my hope with this salon!

**Salon Questionnaire**
> What is something you'd love to accomplish this year? Be as specific as possible.
> Why did you select this idea?
> What are the first three steps you need to take to move this idea forward?
> Who needs to be involved to make this a reality (partner, friend(s), community partner, etc.)?
> What are some challenges you may face, and how might you overcome them?
> List three ways to measure success.

**Breakouts: Questions for Discussion**
> Why did you choose this particular dream to accomplish?
> Why now, and not earlier in your life?
> Do you feel supported by friends, family, and professional colleagues (if applicable) to pursue this goal?
> If not, what allies do you look to for help to keep you moving forward?

## Large Group Discussion

> Is your dream one of attainment or letting go? Or both?
> Do you give yourself permission to fully pursue this dream?
> Is any person or thing (family, money, location, unlikely odds of actually attaining it) getting in your way? Can you address or remedy any of that?

## Closing

We've discussed our dreams for the coming year and written letters to our future selves as a way to check in. We have each other as accountability partners on the journey, should we need that. Think about looking back in a year: What would you be most happy about accomplishing and experiencing? If it's this dream, make it so. Amazing things happen with intention and planning. Let's support each other on our journeys.

## Quotes Selected by Salon Members

"If you want to be happy, set a goal that commands your thoughts, liberates your energy, and inspires your hope." —Andrew Carnegie

"The future belongs to those who believe in the beauty of their dreams." —Eleanor Roosevelt

"A solitary fantasy can transform a million realities." —Maya Angelou

"One cannot collect all the beautiful shells on the beach, one can only collect a few." —Anne Morrow Lindbergh

"The real issue—and it is a spiritual issue—is how we face up . . . to the lifelong and, at times, fierce battle between who we are and who we want to be." —Rabbi Niles Elliot Goldstein

## In Praise of Beauty

When I started my salon, members ranged from their late forties to early eighties, that liminal time when physical beauty, most often associated with youth, feels like it's moving away like a receding tide. Of course, we need to recalibrate our expectations around beauty standards, including our own internal ones. Outside of physical beauty, there are many other kinds to contemplate, like qualities of character, and of course the beauty beyond ourselves, in the world around us. What we consider beautiful is so personal, truly in the eye of the beholder; one person's concept of beauty can be quite different than another's. It was fascinating to talk about this subject and get everyone's take on it. This salon ranked among our favorites and was surprisingly fun and empowering.

### Salon Description

Beauty inspires us; it lifts us up, takes our breath away, or causes us to exhale deeply. Merriam-Webster defines *beauty* as "the quality or aggregate of qualities in a person or thing that gives pleasure to the senses or pleasurably exalts the mind or spirit." Beauty is sensual; I've heard music so beautiful it stopped me in my tracks, touched surfaces so soft I shivered, smelled scents that drew me into another space and time, tasted food that left me speechless, and seen things that blew my mind. Beauty is also commonly associated with women and their loveliness. What do you consider beautiful? Do you think of women as more beautiful than men? Do you think about beauty often, or is it not important to you? Let's talk about what beauty means to each of us.

### Prep Email

Is beauty a quality you think about often? Do you tend to associate your experience of beauty with one sense over another (do you see it more than hear it, etc.)? Over the next week think about what strikes you as beautiful, and why. If you rarely notice beauty, why do you think that is?

**Teaser & Enricher**
Please bring something that exemplifies beauty to you: a picture, a sound recording, a scent, a food, or an object.

**Personal Backstory Shared at Salon**
Over the winter holidays a few years back, I decided to stop highlighting my hair. A visceral reaction upon noticing a lock of grey hair by my temple sparked this decision. I actually jerked away from the mirror, and blinked back tears. How socially conditioned was I to be so shattered by this sign of aging? I didn't like that in myself and resolved to embrace my grey. Five months into this process, when I parted my hair, I saw brown and red, shot through with silver.

Unexpectedly, I found this quite pretty. I did notice a lack of vibrancy, my hair becoming Kansas to its former Oz, but I took comfort that I was sparing my scalp exposure to toxic dyes. I contacted my hair stylist to discuss how I could avoid a potentially jarring grow-out, and visited online support groups for "going grey gracefully." If these groups exist for men, I wasn't seeing them, but for women, the choices were plentiful. Most women don't choose this path and when they do, they receive discouraging comments. I know I did. A few friends pointed out my pale skin and light eyes and suggested I'd look washed out, erased, prematurely aged with grey hair. I wondered, would they say these comments to a man who was considering the same thing? I will never forget a conversation with a woman at my mother's retirement home; she was the daughter of another resident, and shared that she owned a hair salon. I mentioned my decision to stop coloring my hair and she looked at me with the kind of alarm usually reserved for visions of a zombie apocalypse, before asking, "Why would you do that?" What was there about a woman being less color-saturated that brought out a sense of horror in these people? As it turns out, my grey is coming in *very* slowly, and if I'm looking more washed out, so be it. I always have lipstick!

Going grey prompted larger thoughts about beauty and how I define it. Beauty is rarely simple, but always known. It touches my every sense. When I find myself stressed, shallow-breathed, and questioning the meaning of my too-short mortal life, I find solace in beauty. It is there that I ground and find myself again. I open a bag of coffee beans and breathe in its tangy scent, wonder at the spiraling design in the petals of a flower growing in my yard, contemplate the woodland creatures that frequent our deck, or gaze into my dear husband's eyes. When I witness beauty I feel deeply alive and at ease and aware I'm part of something bigger. I feel connected to the universe, to all beings, in a way that's almost trippy. Beauty is a drug that ceaselessly woos me.

## Salon Questionnaire

> Name at least one time you felt really beautiful, and explain why.
> What things, places, or experiences do you associate with beauty?
> Do you tend to associate your experience of beauty with one sense over another (do you see it more than hear it, etc.)?
> When you seek to create beauty, what sense would it appeal to? Please give an example of what you create.

## Breakouts: Questions for Discussion

> Do you actively seek out beauty? If so, in what forms? Music, art, literature, architecture, culinary dishes, natural landscapes, or ones shaped by humans?
> Do you feel called to create beauty? In what ways?
> Does beauty have a gender to you (feel more masculine or feminine)?
> Is there a person who represents beauty to you? Why?

## Large Group Question

> Please share the object you brought that exemplifies beauty and tell us about it.

## Closing

Has our discussion changed any of your feelings around beauty? Because of what we've shared tonight, the tangible and intangible beautiful things that move us, we've reaffirmed that beauty is everywhere, if we open ourselves up to witnessing it in the many forms it may reveal itself.

## Quotes Selected by Salon Members

"At some point in life the world's beauty becomes enough. You don't need to photograph, paint or even remember it. It is enough. No record of it needs to be kept and you don't need someone to share it with or tell it to. When that happens—that letting go—you let go because you can." —Toni Morrison, *Tar Baby*

"The most beautiful people we have known are those who have known defeat, known suffering, known struggle, known loss, and have found their way out of the depths. These persons have an appreciation, a sensitivity, and an understanding of life that fills them with compassion, gentleness, and a deep loving concern. Beautiful people do not just happen." —Elisabeth Kübler-Ross

"Beauty is not in the face; beauty is a light in the heart." —Kahlil Gibran

"The longer I live, the more beautiful life becomes. If you foolishly ignore beauty, then you will soon find yourself without it. Your life will be impoverished. But if you invest in beauty, it will remain with you all the days of your life." —Frank Lloyd Wright

"Beauty awakens the soul to act." —Dante Alighieri

## DREAMS

A dear friend of mine is part of a dream group that meets weekly. They use an approach called the Haden Method. Each person shares a dream they've recently had, describing it without interpreting it. After everyone has shared, the group chooses one or two dreams to discuss. The chosen dreamers describe their dreams one more time. The listeners will then ask the dreamer about any associations that elements and people appearing in the dream might have for them. What feelings come up? What adjectives or other descriptors would they associate with that element or person? Then members ask the dreamer if they can "have" the dream and take it on as if it were their own. Members will internalize the dream aloud, working with the images and actions described through the lens of their own psyches. During this time, the dreamer does not interact or interject, but is simply witness. This method seeks to protect the dreamer and the one taking it on from advice, such as, "you dreamed that because you need to . . .," which can make both parties feel unsafe. And it often yields new insights for the dreamer; we can miss or defend against certain symbolic meanings when we interpret dreams on our own.

My friend shared, "When I first worked like this, it felt a bit awkward, as I was used to being in groups that analyzed each other's dreams. Over time, I came to appreciate the method we now use as it shifts the focus from a reductive analysis to a process that has an enhanced potential to unearth inner elements from each participant."

I wondered how our salon could approach the subject of dreams and meaningfully discuss the impact of our dreams on our waking lives. As usual with our very engaged group, our salon was riveting, at times funny, and in a couple of cases, haunting. I particularly enjoyed the discussion because it offered glimpses into parts of us we hadn't shared before. And for some, it inspired taking a deeper look at their dream lives and journaling.

For this salon's party favor, I purchased soaps scented with lavender, sage, and bergamot essential oils, made especially to aid sleep. I wrapped them in pieces of fabric, tied with twine, and enclosed wishes for sweet dreams in each bundle.

### Salon Description
Carl Jung proposed that dreams are a way for the unconscious mind to communicate with the conscious mind. One of his

most referenced quotes on dreams is from *The Red Book*, "I must learn that the dregs of my thought, my dreams, are the speech of my soul. I must carry them in my heart, and go back and forth over them in my mind, like the words of the person dearest to me. Dreams are the guiding words of the soul." Let's discuss the role of dreams in our lives.

## Prep Email

What part do dreams play in your life? Do you reflect on their possible meanings, or do you tend to dismiss their importance beyond their role as one of the stages of sleep? Did your parents or other caretaker ever discuss dreams with you? Do you think your views on dreams have broader cultural roots?

## Teaser & Enricher

Think about your dreams this week, and if you have a chance, write them down. As we tend to forget dreams quickly, write about them within minutes of waking. How did you feel upon waking? Did you dream in color or black and white? Were you a witness or a participant? Was the dream setting a familiar place? Who was in the dream, and do you know them? Have you had this dream, or a variation of it, before? You do not have to share anything you write at the salon: This is just to prompt you to start thinking more consciously about your dreams.

## Personal Backstory Shared at Salon

Some of us experience vivid dreams every night, while others might not remember their dreams, or insist they don't dream at all. The ancient Greek historian Herodotus reported in his *Histories* about a group of people who lived in North Africa near the mountain called Atlas: "The natives call this mountain 'the Pillar of Heaven' and they themselves take their name from it, being called Atlantes or the Atlanteans. They are reported not to eat any living thing, and never to have any dreams." If you don't think of yourself a dreamer, instead of worrying about a lack of imagination, you might instead consider a connection with the Atlanteans.

Dreams are a nightly experience for me; some dreams recur for decades, others are clearly linked to a specific issue I'm wrestling with, or the result of something I ate, causing strange imaginings or yearnings. I fully inhabit my dreams, though my role can shift from witness to participant. I've wondered if dreams bring us to another plane of existence that we share with others, a collective unconscious where we communicate and journey in ways we cannot in our waking life. I've asked people in my dreams questions that I would not know the answer to, as a test of whether I'm projecting their presence or they are indeed visiting me in my dreamworld. I've also played with a concept a friend shared, that every person in the dream represents ourselves. What does that mean when I look at my dreams with either of these perspectives in mind?

I'm profoundly affected by dreams. During a particularly difficult time, a gentle guardian figure appeared in a dream and told me he would always look out for me. I awoke to wind chimes sounding on the front porch, and felt very safe and cared for in a way that has stayed with me for years. In another dream I was a man, and when I awoke, it took me a few moments to adjust to being in a female body, and reconnect to who I am, to my core identity.

I've always been a prolific dreamer, and regularly have multiple dreams a night, sometimes a run of seemingly unrelated ones, akin to flipping through TV channels with a remote. Or I return to the same dream repeatedly. I've experienced dream paralysis, where I was conscious, but could not move, and have woken myself up from dreams that were very frightening or going in a direction I didn't like for other reasons. I've also practiced lucid dreaming, working with an awareness that I'm in a dream and then shifting the experience and outcome. I might decide I'd like to fly, and then I fly, or if I feel I need to say something to someone, I do. Lucid dreaming can be powerful dreamwork, and I highly recommend giving it a try.

## Salon Questionnaire

> Do you dream? If not, do you ever wonder about that? If you do, how often do you dream, and do you think about your dreams upon waking?
> Supposedly we work out real-life issues in our dreams and can wake up refreshed. Has that ever happened to you? What were you working on?
> Do you believe the theory that every person in the dream is you? How would that affect how you interpret dreams?
> Do you believe in dream telepathy, an ability to communicate with another person while you're both dreaming?

## Breakouts: Questions for Discussion

> Do you remember your dreams upon waking? Do they affect your mood, your approach for the day, or life?
> Do you have the same dreams again and again?
> Have you experienced a superpower in dreams? Flying, breathing underwater, invisibility, an ability to cast spells or wield power in magical ways?
> Do you believe in prophetic dreams? Have you ever had one?

## Large Group Discussion

> Have you ever practiced lucid dreaming or tried to control the outcome of a dream? Did it work?
> Have you ever connected with someone, including someone who was no longer alive, in your dreams? Did it feel real?
> From those who have done a lot of dream work, any insights on the dream world to share with us?

## Closing

Do you feel differently about dreams after this salon discussion? Are they an area of your life that you'd like to track more closely with journaling? Would you like to engage in lucid dreaming? Join a dream group and discuss dreams together? Because so many of us identify as creatives, our dream worlds, and their rich imagery, undoubtedly influence what we create, in ways we may not even be aware of. Dreams can be places where we are most vulnerable, so thank you for sharing from this vulnerable place.

## Quotes Selected by Salon Members

"Dreams are today's answers to tomorrow's questions." —Edgar Cayce

"Dreams are illustrations from the book your soul is writing about you." —Marsha Norman

"I dream my painting and I paint my dream." —Vincent van Gogh

"I think we dream so we don't have to be apart for so long. If we're in each other's dreams, we can be together all the time." —A. A. Milne, *Winnie-the-Pooh*

"Dreams are like letters from God. Isn't it time you answered your mail?" —Marie-Louise von Franz

# WHAT ARE YOU WAITING FOR?

"Tell me, what is it you plan to do with your one wild and
precious life?"
—MARY OLIVER

My workdays are filled with conference calls, fundrais-
ing, bookkeeping, responding to emails, and working
remotely with my team to dream up new ways of bringing
booksellers, publishers, and authors together. Sometimes I
catch myself staring out the window watching birds dart in and
out of the branches of a weeping cherry tree, or neighbors walk
by with their dogs, stopping to browse the latest offerings in
our Little Free Library. I'll push away from the desk every hour
or so to stretch and chat with my husband, a former bookseller and publisher representative who recently retired. For the
most part, though, my daily life is solitary, and connections are
mostly virtual.

But, as a direct result of my salon, I have a special circle of
friends to meet for coffee dates, take in a new movie with, go
for walks around town with, and text to share a funny thing
that happened or the ways a day was unexpectedly hard. A few
of us formed a therapeutic support group during the Covid era,
and it's still going strong. A slightly different grouping went on
our first international trip together to Québec City, which was
mostly splendid except for "that incident at the Strøm Spa,"
which we've resolved never to speak about again, and only
refer to, if we must, while avoiding eye contact and suppress-
ing a giggle or harrumph. The presence and care of my salon

friends have supported me through many changes and been the greatest comfort whenever I'm wrestling with something really sad, or scary, or relentlessly frustrating. We cheer each other on and are champion commiserators. My friends are the best!

While researching for this book, I read many books and articles on building community, combatting loneliness, and the perils of smartphones and social media. Our physical and mental health are deeply affected by the quality and frequency of human connections. Younger generations are reportedly less likely to socialize in person and less likely to enjoy, let alone voluntarily engage in, unscripted, spontaneous conversation. As we move away from in-person interaction, replacing or filtering it through devices and apps, will we eventually forget what we once had, and not even know to mourn it? Or could we instead make a point to embrace in-person connections in whatever ways we can, and create spaces for multigenerational gatherings, to continue this beautiful legacy into the future.

Starting or attending a salon is a simple way to bring these kinds of opportunities into your life and your community. You'll be taking part in a centuries-old tradition of gathering for focused discussion, a tradition that has long been especially important for women, who have routinely been denied the educational opportunities of men and self-educated through intellectual gatherings in their homes. Salons are for everyone, and held in different forms every day around our world. I hope the tips and "lessons learned" from this book inspire you to start your own, or accept an invitation to attend one. I wish you the best of luck in your salon adventures. May they gift you with blessings a hundred times over, as I have been gifted by the Black Swan Salon.

# Resources

*A Black Girl in the Middle: Essays on (Allegedly) Figuring It All Out* by Shenequa Golding, Beacon Press, 2024, 978-080700798-3

*A Field Guide to Getting Lost* by Rebecca Solnit, Penguin, 2006, 978-0143037248

*A House Full of Daughters: A Memoir of Seven Generations* by Juliet Nicolson, Farrar, Straus and Giroux, 2019, 09780374172459

*Daring Greatly: How the Courage to Be Vulnerable Transforms the Way We Live, Love, Parent, and Lead* by Brené Brown, Avery, 2015, 978-1-592-40841-2

*Fed Up: Emotional Labor, Women, and the Way Forward* by Gemma Hartley, HarperOne, 2018, 978-0-06-285598-5

*Find Your People: Building Deep Community in a Lonely World* by Jennie Allen, WaterBrook, 2022, 978-0-593-19338-9

*Friendship* by A. C. Grayling, Yale University Press, 2014, 9780300205367

*Friendshipping: The Art of Finding Friends, Being Friends, and Keeping Friends* by Jenn Bane and Trin Garritano, Workman Publishing, 2020, 978-1-5235-0861-7

"Get the Facts on Women and Aging" by the National Council on Aging, accessed February 25, 2025, https://www.ncoa.org/article/get-the-facts-on-women-and-aging/

*Hanging Out: The Radical Power of Killing Time* by Sheila Liming, Melville House, 2023, 978-1-68589-005-6

211

*How to Know a Person: The Art of Seeing Others Deeply and Being Deeply Seen* by David Brooks, Random House, 2023, 978-0593-230060

*How We Got to Now: Six Innovations That Made the Modern World* by Steven Johnson, Riverhead, 2015, 978-1594633935

*In Montmartre: Picasso, Matisse and the Birth of Modernist Art* by Sue Roe, Penguin, 2014, 978-1-59420-495-1

*Joyful: The Surprising Power of Ordinary Things to Create Extraordinary Happiness* by Ingrid Fetell Lee, Little, Brown Spark, 2018, 978-0-316-39926-5

*Life Admin: How I Learned to Do Less, Do Better, and Live More* by Elizabeth Emens, HarperOne, 2019, 978-0-544-55723-9

*Playing Big: Practical Wisdom for Women Who Want to Speak Up, Create, and Lead* by Tara Mohr, Avery, 2014, 978-1-592-40960-0

*Reclaiming Conversation: The Power of Talk in a Digital Age* by Sherry Turkle, Penguin, 2015, 9781594205552

*Talking Cure: An Essay on the Civilizing Power of Conversation* by Paula Marantz Cohen, Princeton University Press, 2023, 9780691238500

*The Age of Insight: The Quest to Understand the Unconscious in Art, Mind, and Brain, From Vienna 1900 to the Present* by Eric R. Kandel, Random House, 2012, 978-1-4000-6871-5

*The Art of Gathering: How We Meet and Why It Matters* by Priya Parker, Riverhead, 2018, 978-1-59463-492-5

*The Nine Lives of Pakistan: Dispatches from a Precarious State* by Declan Walsh, W. W. Norton, 2020, 9780393249910

*The Power of Regret: How Looking Backward Moves Us Forward* by Daniel H. Pink, Riverhead, 2022, 978-0735210653

*Together: The Healing Power of Human Connection in a Sometimes Lonely World* by Vivek H. Murthy, Harper, 2020, 978-006-291329-6

"Trends in AARP Research on Women" by AARP, accessed February 25, 2025, https://www.aarp.org/pri/topics/aging-experience/demographics/aarp-research-women-trends/

*Where Good Ideas Come From: The Natural History of Innovation* by Steven Johnson, Riverhead, 2011, 978-1594485381

*Why We Can't Sleep: Women's New Midlife Crisis* by Ada Calhoun, Grove Press, 2021, 9780802148575

# Acknowledgments

When I began this project, I wrote "Make It Beautiful" on a Post-it and stuck it on my computer monitor. These three words became my mantra as I wove the story of the Black Swans into instructions for readers who seek to create their own salon. This writing journey has been the deepest pleasure for me, mining personal history, interviewing the Black Swans, and reading many books and articles on communication, socializing, entertaining, and the history of salons and other kinds of gatherings. I'm so very grateful for the opportunity to share this book with readers.

The inspiration for this book grew out of a series of conversations with my sister, Diane Barrett Tien about my experiences hosting the Black Swan Salon. She suggested I write about it, and has been supportive and encouraging from day one. Thank you, Diane!

Thank you to Laura Stanfill, publisher of Forest Avenue Press, for helping me in the early days of this project, and to Nicki Leone, for her patience and skill turning my word doc into a professionally formatted proposal.

Thank you to my dear friends, writer and poet Maria Fire, and writer and artist Constance Lombardo, for reading and offering insightful recommendations on multiple drafts. I am indebted to you both!

Thank you to the members of my women's group and to

my friends Tim and Margaret Callahan, who listened and cheered me on during writing challenges. I'm very appreciative of The Secret Gardeners, a local writing group, for their feedback early on.

A big-hearted thank you to the kind folks at Agate Publishing, including mentor and believer Doug Seibold, editors Marta Evans and Amanda Gibson, production manager Jane Seibold, publicity manager Jacqueline Jarik, and designer Morgan Krehbiel. Working with you has been a delight from the beginning, and I'm proud to be published by you. Your support of this project has fulfilled a life-long dream. I'm thrilled that the PGW/Ingram sales team will be supporting my book's launch. They are the best sales team on the planet!

So much gratitude to my husband, Jon Mayes, who was my emotional support human throughout the entire writing process. He was there for me in whatever ways I needed.

And a huge thank you and hug to the members of the Black Swan Salon: Clara Boza, Annice Brown, Sarah Corley, Lockie Hunter, Constance Lombardo, Donna McCalman, Laurie Miller, Ryn Potter, and the others past, present, and future. You can hear their voices among these pages, as I keep them in my heart. May we continue to grow this beautiful thing we've created together.

# INDEX

# About the Author

LINDA-MARIE BARRETT is a writer, editor, and executive director of the Southern Independent Booksellers Alliance (SIBA). She has been hosting her Black Swan Salon since 2017 and has no plans to ever stop. She has a BA in Russian Studies from Colgate University, and an MA in Russian Literature and Slavic Linguistics from Cornell University, where she received a National Resource Fellowship and an Olin Fellowship. From 1988–2017, she worked at Malaprop's Bookstore/Cafe, where she wore many hats, including author events manager, general manager, and co-owner. She edited and contributed to the regional bestselling serial novel *Naked Came the Leaf Peeper*, called "a blur, a buzz, a local-grown tall tale, and an absolute delight" by Elizabeth Gilbert, and contributed to *Spinning Toward the Sun: Essays on Writing, Resilience, and the Creative Life*, an anthology benefitting the recovery of Asheville, North Carolina, after Hurricane Helene. She lives with her husband, writer and blogger Jon Mayes, in Asheville, and writes a blog at Barrett-Sisters.com with her sister, Diane Barrett Tien, where they share about life's curveballs and rewards. Please visit her online at lindamariebarrett.com.